ATLANTA'S
DRUID HILLS

ATLANTA'S

DRUID HILLS

A BRIEF HISTORY

ROBERT HARTLE JR.

Charleston   London
THE
History
PRESS

Published by The History Press
Charleston, SC 29403
www.historypress.net

First published 2008
Second printing 2008

Manufactured in the United States

ISBN 978.1.59629.375.5

Library of Congress Cataloging-in-Publication Data

Hartle, Robert.
Atlanta's Druid Hills : a brief history / Robert Hartle.
p. cm.
Includes bibliographical references.
ISBN 978-1-59629-375-5
1. Druid Hills (Atlanta, Ga.)--History. 2. Real estate development--Georgia--Atlanta--History. 3. Olmsted,
Frederick Law, 1822-1903. 4. Hurt, Joel, 1850-1926. 5. Emory University.--History. I. Title.
F294.A86D784 2008
975.8'231--dc22

2008005095

Dedicated to my parents for all their help and support throughout the years.

Contents

Acknowledgements

Many thanks to Charles E. Beveridge, series editor of the Frederick Law Olmsted Papers Project, for his encouragement and his very helpful comments on the manuscript; to Mrs. Alida Silverman for her very helpful comments; and to Joanna Stroud for her assistance.

Big thanks for the interview: William R. Mitchell; Dr. Sally West and Dr. Daniel Pollock; Dr. Dana F. White; Dr. Marion Kuntz; Commissioner Pete and Mrs. Gerry Wheeler; Martha Manning; Patsy Guy; and Susan Summers.

Big thanks for the advice/help: Lynn Speno; Dr. Donald and Mrs. Molly Verene; the DHCA; staff of the Dekalb Historical Society; staff of the Atlanta History Center; staff of Georgia State University Special Collections; staff of Emory University Special Collections; staff of Georgia Department of Archives; Nunan Family; Lee Handford; Marshall Hudson.

Big thanks for the encouragement: Aunt Judy; Marcey Hoelting; David Lewis; Chris Jones; Will Thompson; Evelyn-Anne Johnston; The Miz; Sky Lawyer; all my friends in Dallas; Mr. and Mrs. Sarah Brittingham; and you, for buying this book.

Special thanks to Dr. Sally West and Dr. Daniel Pollock for access to the letter about their home, which appears in Chapter Four.

Introduction

Olmsted's masterpiece, to my mind, is the little known but exquisite estate of trees, lakes, lawns and rolling hills, encompassing Emory University bang in the middle of Atlanta, Ga.
—*Alistair Cooke,* The Americans

Cooke's storied writing and broadcasting career included a period as host of *Omnibus*, CBS's first series, beginning in 1952, to be devoted to the arts. It was here that Jessica Tandy revived her original Broadway performance as the character Blanche DuBois. However, not until some thirty-five years later would she find her greatest critical acclaim in *Driving Miss Daisy*, set and filmed in the neighborhood Cooke called "Olmsted's Masterpiece."

Even a *New York Times* reporter took notice while scouting the city before the 1996 Olympics. Comparing Druid Hills with the fashionable Buckhead neighborhood, he wrote:

> *Just as lovely on the east side of town near Emory University is the Druid Hills area, where the film* Driving Miss Daisy *was shot and the real Miss Daisy lived. Frederick Law Olmsted designed some of the small parks in the area, with their rolling hills and manicured greenery. Druid Hills meanders off Ponce de Leon Avenue and is best exemplified by its grand, rambling houses built near the beginning of the century on shady streets such as Lullwater, Oakdale and Springdale Roads.*[1]

Long before it was placed on the National Register of Historic places in 1979, Druid Hills was home to settlers who had moved from the Carolinas—such as Naman Hardman, who built the Hardman Cemetery in 1825. The cemetery, though not the Baptist church that once stood beside it, still exists on land belonging to Emory University's Clairmont

Campus. The church, along with much of Atlanta, was burned by Sherman in 1864 after he had used it as a field hospital following the battle for Decatur.[2]

While preservation efforts for the cemetery succeeded, other pre–Druid Hills landmarks are long gone. One of these was a "medicine house," owned and operated by Dr. Chapmon Powell, located at the intersection of North Decatur and Clairmont Roads. Once upon a time, both whites and Native Americans were given medical treatment in an area now occupied by strip malls.[3]

Powell's log cabin practice was moved here after his son-in-law W.J. Houston purchased about five hundred acres of his land. Hahn Woods lies off Houston Mill Road at the spot where Houston transformed his plantation's mill into the area's first electric-powered generation plant. This occurred in 1905, more than forty years after Federal Fourth Corps troops crossed the south fork of Peachtree Creek at Durand Mill on July 20, 1864, en route through the city to the sea. Two days prior, skirmishing had gone on at Clairmont and North Decatur, near the Powell House, which served as Sherman's headquarters on July 19.[4]

In 1821, Native Americans surrendered the land now known as Druid Hills to the Georgia government, which surveyed it into plots of 202.5 acres. Drawings for the land were then held for Georgia residents. Over time, John Gerdine Johnson accumulated most of the land surrounding what are now Ponce de Leon Avenue and Briarcliff, North Decatur and Lullwater Roads. By the time Joel Hurt purchased all but ten acres from Johnson's surviving family in 1890, Atlanta was in its rebuilding period. What Hurt was able to recognize, before most others, was that Atlanta would rebuild at a staggering rate, and the need for residential neighborhoods near the city would soon be in vogue and very much in demand.

Chapter 1

Designing According to Nature

Joel Hurt and Frederick Law Olmsted

In an *Atlanta Constitution* article dated June 3, 1905, the author—although he does not specifically refer to it—describes the eighteenth-century European debate between the carefully structured, geometrical French landscape ideal, and the free-flowing, "let man build around nature while taking as few liberties as possible" British landscape ideal, which was the current trend in America.

> [In the courtly French gardens] *there were flower beds bordered with designs in dwarf box, upon which the aspiring youth might demonstrate a theorem in geometry or perhaps cross the pons asinorum. But the modern school of art has changed all this, and architecture out of doors no more follows the conventional lines of Euclid, nor are the flowers expected to bloom into theorems. In the best of architecture, otherwise known as landscape gardening, nature has her own sweet will....Now the house nestles in the landscape as naturally as if it had grown there and no barbarism of a geometrical flower bed or conical hedge is allowed to startle the eye with the painful suggestion of engineering diagrams, where the repose of nature invited you to leave off toil and enter into rest.* [5]

The article from which the above extract was taken was written before Druid Hills had even been developed, yet its author is convinced that the only place comparable to it in terms of beauty and diversity of plant life is the Vanderbilt arboretum at Biltmore. That is probably the highest compliment one could pay, coming from the modern school of thought, since the Vanderbilt arboretum at Biltmore was one of the few places in the South designed by the "father of landscape architecture" Frederick Law Olmsted. Obviously the author picked up on these similarities, since the Olmsted brothers—Frederick Law Olmsted Jr. (Olmsted's son) and John Charles Olmsted (Olmsted's stepson)—designed the original plan. At the time, "Renaissance Man" Joel Hurt was Atlanta's most progressive developer, intent on uniting the arts with business and owning a keen eye for predicting future trends.

In 1890, Hurt began a courtship of Olmsted that would indelibly link him to the founding of Druid Hills.

Joel Hurt was born on July 31, 1850, in Hurtsboro, Alabama. Hurt was not wealthy, but he was able to matriculate at Auburn University for one year before finishing his education at Franklin College (now the University of Georgia) in Athens, Georgia. He graduated in 1871 with a civil engineering degree. From there, Hurt spent the next four years working as a railroad surveyor in different parts of the country before relocating to Atlanta in 1875. A jack-of-all-trades if ever there was one, Hurt would spend the next fifty years involved in everything from insurance to streetcars, to botany and horticulture.

Hurt's first undertaking was alongside his brother in E.F. (Elisha Fletcher) and Joel Hurt, an insurance and real estate firm. The name would soon change to Hurt and Low when Elisha left the rebuilding city of Atlanta for New York and was replaced by James Low. Soon after, Hurt sold the company and formed the Atlanta Home Insurance Company.

Hurt was also a major promoter of the electric streetcar. In 1891, he consolidated six different electric streetcar lines, creating the Atlanta Consolidated Street Railway Company. Just two years earlier, Hurt had financed Atlanta's first streetcar line, which ran along Edgewood Avenue with one end stopping downtown and the other stopping at Inman Park, Atlanta's first residential suburb.

In 1886, Hurt founded the East Atlanta Land Company, through which he surveyed and developed Edgewood Avenue and Inman Park. One criticism of Hurt throughout his career was that he would, often without proper funding, dive headfirst into a project only to abandon it shortly thereafter.[6] Judging by the massive number of projects he undertook, and their magnitude, it is no surprise that Hurt was forced to abandon some and therefore could come across like a child who begs and begs for a new toy and then grows tired of it after a few hours. However, while he may have been prone to jumping the gun on business endeavors, it would be hard to overstate his influence on post–Civil War Atlanta.

As one admirer believes:

> *Joel Hurt was so far ahead of the times and the section of the country in which he lived, that the progress he made more often than not had to be accomplished single handed...It was because of the energy and progressiveness of such men as Joel Hurt...that the south recovered as rapidly as it did.[7]*

Atlanta was certainly recovering remarkably fast. In 1870, the post–Civil War depredation to Atlanta was clear as its population stood just under twenty-two thousand people. Just twenty years later, the population had tripled to approximately sixty-six thousand.[8] Hurt's awareness of the continued population growth, combined with the success of Atlanta's first residential suburb, Inman Park, and his increasing interest in botany, impelled Hurt to organize the Kirkwood Land Company with plans to construct a new residential neighborhood northeast of the city.

At the time, landscapes were moving away from restrictive geometrical confines intent on shaping the environment and toward a free-flowing adherence to the land's natural layout.

The man most closely associated with this movement—whose work Hurt was very familiar with—was Brookline, Massachusetts–based landscape architect Frederick Law Olmsted.

Several factors contributed to the partnership formed between Hurt and Olmsted. First, Olmsted had a great interest in the South, having made many visits to different states and recording his observations in numerous volumes of journals. At the time he became associated with Hurt, Olmsted was nearing the end of his professional life and had a sincere interest in seeing a reunified United States. Olmsted's intentions are made clear in an 1894 letter to his stepson John C. Olmsted:

> *I want the firm to have an established "good will" in the South. Then, as we would all be called abolitionists in the South, I think a demonstration that the time has passed in which hatred of abolitionists is an element of consequence in matters of professional business is of some value.*[9]

Secondly, Olmsted had recently designed the grounds for George Washington Vanderbilt II's Biltmore Estate in Asheville, North Carolina, and was interested in pursuing additional projects in the South. Furthermore, his help had been solicited in the planning of the Cotton States and International Exposition, which took place in 1895 in what is now Atlanta's Piedmont Park. (The event was a showcase of sorts for Southeastern businesses and technologies. Almost 800,000 people attended, and the event drew national attention after Booker T. Washington gave his legendary "Atlanta Compromise" speech.)

Though Olmsted and Hurt could not have been raised in more different environments— Hurt grew up in rural Alabama and was still a boy at the start of the Civil War, while Olmsted was raised in Hartford, Connecticut, and was a grown man and ardent abolitionist by that time—Elizabeth A. Lyon notes similarities between the two: "Both men were civil engineers who developed an enthusiasm for landscape design and a concern for a healthful environment." And both men could instinctively "see the trends of future changes and developments."[10]

Despite these similarities between the two men, and a mutual interest in Atlanta's development, Hurt and Olmsted's partnership never fully materialized, primarily as a result of the increasing financial woes Hurt experienced in his many business ventures. The Panic of 1893—brought on when the Federal Reserve reached its minimum on gold that could be redeemed for silver notes, resulting in inflated interest payments on government bonds— caused widespread bankruptcy throughout the country and forced Hurt to temporarily abandon plans for Druid Hills in order to concentrate on business ventures to which he was more financially committed.

By 1895, not only had his body weakened, but Olmsted also began to notice significant memory loss.[11] The combination was enough to officially retire the "father of landscape architecture" seven years before Hurt was able to resume work on Druid Hills. While Olmsted was never able to see the project through, in 1893 he and John C. Olmsted did prepare a plan for what is now essentially the Ponce de Leon Avenue district of Druid Hills. This plan laid out the shape of Ponce de Leon and the linear parks, the parkland in the valleys of Peavine Creek and the roads. Though it is easy to overstate Olmsted's role in Druid Hills' development, the Ponce de Leon area could not be more emblematic of Olmstedian design.

Darlene R. Roth notes the three components essential to Olmsted's ideal suburb:

> [First, the] *park or public space element, which was the central focus of the suburb, and served as the "drawing card" to make it more than an ordinary place. The second component was the parkway, conceived as both a connector and a pleasure drive, which linked the suburb with the nearby city, and provided a pleasurable experience for the commuter. The final component comprised the residential buildings, which took the form of "villas," constructed on large lots.*[12]

Over a hundred years after Olmsted chose the area now known as Ponce de Leon for development, these three principles can be easily seen. Deepdene and Springdale are two examples of the six parks sequentially linked alongside Ponce de Leon Avenue that provide recreation with walking paths, picnic areas and so on.[13] Such was of the utmost importance to Olmsted, as the ideal neighborhood would not only provide shelter and accessible transportation routes, but also aesthetically pleasing recreational areas that allowed for reflection and relaxation after a long day's work.

Parallel to the line of parks sit grandiose mansions—many of which have been converted to church buildings or other nonresidential facilities—each with its own unique design and separated by substantial yards, a far cry from the cramped, "you've seen one you've seen 'em all" subdivisions of today. Finally, the parkway—Ponce de Leon Avenue—typifies Olmsted's belief that a "curvilinear street pattern"[14] was essential for adhering to the natural topography of the rolling hills found in the ideal suburb.

Describing his vision for the parkway, which would connect Druid Hills with downtown Atlanta, Olmsted wrote in a letter to Joel Hurt:

> *The Parkway should be as spacious as circumstances will permit; and should be finely constructed, and adequate arrangements should be made for lots being well shaded by handsome, umbrageous, permanently thrifty trees.*[15]

During the first half of the twentieth century, when Druid Hills was home to the elite of Atlanta's "movers and shakers," Ponce de Leon Avenue was the home to many of the city's biggest names, such as Candler, Arkwright and Adair, and it exemplified what the suburb was designed to offer, namely "the contrast of gracefully-curved lines, sylvan beauty, tranquility, and wholesome domesticity," all of which counteracted the "tension, impersonality, and alienation which are the psychosocial symptoms of the commercial preoccupations of the city."[16]

In 1902, when Joel Hurt was financially capable of turning his interest back to suburban development, it was Olmsted's stepson John C. Olmsted with whom he would be dealing. Still, the next few years saw sporadic development, as Hurt was often preoccupied with other business ventures. For a brief time it appeared as if Hurt would be able to see the project through. The year 1905 was highlighted by the Olmsted brothers' completion of the plan for Druid Hills. Two years later, the Kirkwood Land Company landscaped the surrounding land, developed the thoroughfare and sectioned off lots on what is now the Ponce de Leon corridor. Unfortunately, this was the last hurrah for the Kirkwood Land Company, as Joel Hurt sold its landholdings in 1908 to a group of investors composed of Asa Candler, Forrest and George Adair and Preston Arkwright. This group would ultimately oversee the completion of what became Druid Hills. However, for roughly seventeen years, it was largely Joel Hurt's vision and determination that kept the wheels turning in the development of this "ideal residential suburb."

Chapter 2

The Druid Hills Company

The Millionaire Colony

THIS is the forest primeval. The murmuring pines and the hemlocks,
Bearded with moss, and in garments green, indistinct in the twilight,
Stand like Druids of eld, with voices sad and prophetic,
Stand like harpers hoar, with beards that rest on their bosoms.
—Longfellow, "Evangeline"

Any educated man in the early twentieth century was familiar with Longfellow, so this quote from "Evangeline" was about as good an explanation as I could find for why John C. Olmsted suggested the name Druid Hills. In fact, Druid Hills was suggested because the area reminded him of Druid Hill Park in Baltimore, Maryland. The name was chosen by Joel Hurt in 1902 after reviewing a list, compiled by Olmsted, of thirty-nine possible names.[17] Druid Hill Park was likely named by Colonel Nicholas Rogers upon his return to Baltimore after studying at Glasgow University in Scotland. As Eden Unger Bowditch notes, the Druids had "veneration for nature and, in particular, oaks, tops of hills and certain groves of trees." Furthermore, oaks represented the spiritual and physical well-being of Celtic clans. An oak was planted in the center of each clan's courtyard, and if a rival clan disfigured or destroyed it, that was a sign of total defeat. The land that makes up Druid Park is characterized by rolling hills and numerous oaks, hence the name.[18]

The National Park Service describes Druid Hills' boundaries as follows:

Druid Hills is roughly bounded by the Fulton County line on the west, Briarcliff Rd. to the northwest, just over the Emory Rd. line on the north and following the southside of Emory Rd. The boundary cuts south and juts east around the Fernbank Forest and Recreational Center, then cuts east and south along tracks of the Seaboard Coast Line. South it is bordered by North Ave. and the Atlanta City Boundary.

A syndicate composed of Asa Candler, realtors Forrest and George Adair and Georgia Railway and Electric Company president Preston Arkwright purchased the holdings of the Kirkwood Company in May of 1908. The holdings totaled 1,492 acres and cost $.5 million dollars.[19] The syndicate came together for its first meeting on June 30, 1908, after being granted a corporate charter by the DeKalb County Superior Court.

The corporation was divided into 2,500 shares of stock valued at $200 per share. Candler was the company's dominant shareholder with 2,250 shares; the Adairs purchased 25 shares; Arkwright, 125; attorney Harold Hirsch, 25; William D. Thompson, 25; and Judge John S. Candler, 50. In addition, the Adairs were named as the sole realtors for the property. Research has shown the Adairs to be fairly interesting characters. If I had to describe them based on my research, I would say they were "extremely savvy." By 1928, a host of lawsuits were being filed, claiming that the Adair Realty and Trust Company had purposely issued fraudulent bonds, and according to an *Atlanta Constitution* report, when the company went bankrupt on March 31, 1927, their "liabilities listed at $40,000,000."[20] No matter the outcome of their company, the Adairs proved invaluable in attracting high-end clientele to Druid Hills.

Forrest and George Adair ran what was Atlanta's oldest realty company, started by their father Colonel George W. Adair immediately following the Civil War.[21] Charles Howard Candler, like many others who dealt with them, did not trust the Adairs any farther than he could throw them. In his biography of his father Asa Candler, he claimed that the Adairs used his father for a "free ride." From this distance, he appears to be correct. In May of 1910, Asa Candler agreed to put up the money for the Adairs' newly formed Realty Investments Incorporated to purchase real estate titles for what became Druid Hills. The terms of this agreement left all the risk to Candler, and only half of the reward, as profits were to be divided equally between himself and the Adairs. However, if the Adairs' real estate speculation were to end up "in the red," Candler would incur the entire loss.[22] Asa Candler did not share his son's opinion of the Adairs, as is evident in the fact that he appointed Forrest Adair as campaign manager for his 1916 mayoral campaign.[23]

Regardless of any character issues the Adairs may or may not have had, they were shrewd realtors who succeeded in attracting some of the most prominent Georgians. There is no finer example than governor Hoke Smith. Smith served as U.S. secretary of state from 1893 to 1896 before becoming governor of Georgia in 1907. In February of 1909, the *Atlanta Constitution* announced that the Adair brothers sold three lots to Smith at a reported cost of $16,950. The first lot was to feature a $25,000 home, designed for the governor by architect Harry Leslie Walker. Another would feature a home designed and lived in by architect Ronald Ransom, who had recently married the governor's daughter. Numerous other sales were announced, including Forrest Adair's and Preston Arkwright's purchase of double lots, valued at $14,000 and $16,500 respectively.[24]

No time was wasted after the purchase of Druid Hills. Within the first few months following the sale, about $100,000 in contracts were negotiated for improvements on the land, including an eight-inch water main, which ran from Ponce de Leon Spring to Lullwater Road, and a separate sewer system for the neighborhood, as well as contracts

Forrest Adair spends time with a sick child outside Scottish Rite Hospital in 1915. *Courtesy of the Vanishing Georgia Collection, Georgia Division of Archives and History.*

with Atlanta Gas Light Company and advertisements for paving the roadways. (The Druid Hills Corporation was intent on doing away with the dust created by passing motorists as soon as possible.)

The company also hired D.F. Thompson to construct a bridge across Lullwater Creek in order to provide a direct route to the East Lake Club. The first home built in Druid Hills was for Judge Candler. It was a one-story bungalow, erected in 1909 along Ponce de Leon Avenue on approximately four hundred square feet of land.[25] It was built by architect G.L. Norrman and designed in a "French Renaissance mode."[26]

In 1910, Forrest Adair purchased another eighty acres, slightly over half of which were within the city limits of Decatur. An *Atlanta Constitution* article predicted the following, all of which would come to fruition:

> *This land deal means that at no distant date the Druid Hills improvement will extend all the way to Decatur: that Ponce de Leon avenue will be graded, and most probably that Decatur will be joined to Atlanta by a most beautiful residence section…The grading of Ponce de Leon avenue, according to Mr. Adair, will make one of the most splendid drives within the limits of the county.[27]*

In 1909, Forrest Adair claimed that the Druid Hills Corporation would continue development in the Olmsted spirit. As Elizabeth A. Lyon notes, while the Druid Hills Corporation failed in many ways to follow the Kirkwood Company's plans, the area along Ponce de Leon Avenue comprising "its large lots, parks, and landscaped setting…reflects the Olmsted influence."[28]

Improvements continued steadily for the next decade—including the construction of an electric street railway along Ponce de Leon Avenue in 1913—and in the 1920s Druid Hills would establish itself as the home for Atlanta's "movers and shakers." The year 1919 ended the decade on a high note for the blossoming neighborhood when it was announced that St. Elmo Massengale, president of the extremely successful Massengale Advertising Agency, would build a home in Druid Hills.[29] Also that year, Forrest Adair sold his own home to James D. Robinson and made plans to build another stately residence along Springdale Road.[30]

By 1920, real estate records were being shattered throughout the state. The Adairs were raking in so much money that, upon being granted a charter, they took the company public in 1920 with a capital stock of $2 million.[31] Business was so good that in 1921 Forrest Adair, who along with his brother George was active in many other facets of business, removed himself from all business dealings not directly related to real estate. An *Atlanta Constitution* article from March 27, 1921, described the reputation Mr. Adair had earned:

> *There is no man perhaps in Atlanta who has a greater knowledge of real estate and realty values than has Mr. Adair, and he has taken part in many of the biggest deals and developments recorded in the history of the city.*

As noted earlier, Forrest Adair, prior to limiting his business endeavors solely to real estate, resembled Hurt insofar as he enjoyed varied business interests. Another quality he shared with the multitalented Hurt was an ability for predicting future trends—in this case concerning realty. He speculated in 1923:

> *There is every reason for confidence in the future development of the south and of Atlanta, for extensive building operations are undertaken only when people are prosperous—and southern people are prosperous now to a marked degree—as also evidently are many of the people of Atlanta.*[32]

Adair himself was prosperous beyond a marked degree, and he continued to impress onlookers by commissioning more grandiose homes in what had recently been dubbed "Atlanta's millionaire colony."[33]

Four years later, an article appeared in the *Atlanta Constitution* that supported Adair's claim that Atlanta realty was on the rise. The article also asserted that Druid Hills was a barometer for Atlanta real estate.

> *Similar to the part played by steel on the stock exchange as a barometer of the entire market, lot sales in Druid Hills, one of Atlanta's most substantial subdivisions, serve as an excellent indicator of the general residential market, which reveals outstanding prosperity in view of the recent announcement of C.F. Wilkinson, manager of the Druid Hills sales office, to the effect that record sales and resales are being enjoyed.*
>
> *The fact that real estate offices throughout the city are reporting active conditions in the field of homes and residential lots since the first of the year [1926] seems to strengthen the value of Druid Hills sales as a market barometer. On repeated occasions the trend towards an active market has been forecast by increased sales in Druid Hills.*
>
> *"While Druid Hills has always drawn a healthy volume of business," Mr. Wilkinson remarked, "there are, of course, periodical fluctuations other than those due to seasonal changes. The steady growth of Druid Hills along the high ideals originally aimed at has resulted in a general growth of sales volume which tends to increase at a rate dependent on market conditions, but always to increase."*
>
> *From the present volume of sales and resales of residential property in Druid Hills there is every reason to believe that the general real estate market is good. With the close of 1926 as one of the best renting years prevailing in this section for some time, it was predicted that a prosperous residential sales year was due for 1927. From what can be observed from this office, that prediction has been more than substantiated. Besides the sales activity that has been most gratifying to this organization, proof of the heavy demand for homes can be seen in the heavy construction now under way in Druid Hills.*[34]

The purpose of including the preceding article is not simply to verify the statements Adair made four years earlier, but also to show how important Druid Hills had become in the greater picture of Atlanta. By making statements such as the above, Wilkinson links Druid Hills indelibly with Atlanta as a whole. Therefore, anyone reading this article in

1927 could come to no rational conclusion other than that Druid Hills was the preeminent Atlanta neighborhood. As Druid Hills prospered or declined, so would Atlanta residential neighborhoods en bloc.

Druid Hills, by the late 1920s, was renowned around Atlanta as a first-class neighborhood, and with the advent of the "Homes Beautiful" tour, people from all over the southeast would become familiar with the "millionaire colony."[35] The tour, which began in 1924 and showcased many of Atlanta's finest residences, showed a consistent increase in annual attendance. Many of the years—including 1926 when over a hundred thousand people attended the eight-day event—Druid Hills' homes left the jaws of folks from different areas of the Southeast agape.[36]

With all of the publicity Druid Hills was garnering as Atlanta's "millionaire colony," crime in the neighborhood began to increase as burglars began to take notice. Accordingly, the need for police protection became an issue. Druid Hills residents were able to negotiate with the DeKalb County Commission for the Druid Hills area outside Atlanta city limits to be patrolled by DeKalb County Police, effective April 1, 1928.[37]

The following year, a bus line was authorized to run from the intersection of Ponce de Leon Avenue and Clifton Road to the Decatur courthouse and Georgia railroad depot. The Inter-City Coach Company, instead of the Georgia Power Company, was given the rights to operate this line.[38]

In 1928, with the increase in the number of families now living in Druid Hills, plans were made to erect a permanent building for the Druid Hills School, which was founded by Emory University in 1919 and was temporarily located in the university's Fishburne building. The school was chartered for the children of Emory faculty, and therefore it was Emory that funded the construction of the new building, designed by the firm of Ivey and Crook. The result was an elegant, red brick building, built in the style that defined Ivey and Crook's work at the time, described by historian William R. Mitchell Jr. as "the textbook definition of classicism: clearness, elegance, symmetry, and repose produced by attention to traditional forms, and admiration for Greek and Roman models."[39]

Druid Hills now had in place police protection, reliable methods of transportation and an educational system. One thing still lacking was reliable defense against fire. In April of 1933, the only residences in Druid Hills whose calls would be answered by the Atlanta fire department were those whose proprietors had pledged fifty dollars to the fire department. Basically, if one failed to pledge the fifty dollars and one's house caught fire, one was left to one's own devices to extinguish the blaze.[40] For the reason stated, along with complaints of unfair taxation, Druid Hills petitioned to incorporate into DeKalb County in 1933. Druid Hills was the only unincorporated area of DeKalb County, and if its petition was granted, Druid Hills would become its own city between Atlanta and Decatur. As a result, it would be subject to taxation from DeKalb County, which would prove to be far less costly than the taxes it paid at the time.

Members of the Druid Hills charter committee—including some of Atlanta's financial heavyweights, such as Charles Howard Candler and W.D. Thomson (John S. Candler's law partner)—raised the issue that, according to their figures, Druid Hills was annually paying

Street Scene in Druid Hills, Atlanta, Ga.

Courtesy of the Joe Lee Collection, DeKalb History Center.

$16,000 more to the county treasury than it received back for its schools. These factors led the committee to propose a charter for incorporation, with the following expectation:

> *Savings in fire insurance premiums alone will not only maintain the fire department and pay all other salaries required for operation of the municipality, but will yield in addition substantial savings to residents of the area. Under the proposed charter it is impossible for taxes to be levied at a rate any higher than that prevailing heretofore. As a matter of fact, these taxes will be substantially less. The plan also provides a safe guarantee against annexation of the area by Atlanta or Decatur.[41]*

Initial results indicated that Druid Hills was on its way to becoming a city when the Georgia Senate voted to pass the bill. Unfortunately for the bill's supporters, a plea was made by Senator Walter A. Sims to Governor Eugene Talmadge urging him to veto the bill. Sims, upset that the bill was passed on a day when he was absent from the Senate, proved successful when Governor Talmadge vetoed the bill. The governor gave two reasons for his decision. First, he argued that the primary effect of Druid Hills becoming its own city would be the hindrance to Atlanta's expansion. Talmadge was of the opinion that, since the majority of Druid Hills residents worked in Atlanta, if their intent was to live in an incorporated city, why not incorporate into Atlanta and help enlarge the city that was paramount to their livelihoods?

The second reason given for vetoing the bill had to do with a provision within the bill stating that the three Druid Hills school commissioners would sit on the Atlanta city commission for the initial two years of incorporation. Simply put, Talmadge disagreed with the principle that Druid Hills ought to have the authority to appoint city officials.[42]

Despite the failed attempt at incorporation, Druid Hills succeeded in resolving its fire protection issues. On March 18, the state legislature voted 160 to none in favor of an amendment allowing DeKalb County to build and run a fire station in Druid Hills. The bill was handled by Augustine Sams—a state representative who was also a member of the Druid Hills charter committee during its attempt at incorporation—and provided county-run fire protection, which required all Druid Hills residents to pay a yearly tax. The move toward county fire protection was a welcomed one, as it insured that all residents would pay for and receive fire protection.[43]

County fire protection naturally made Druid Hills even more appealing to potential residents. Another area of appeal at the time was a variety of high-end social events and entertainment opportunities, at least on par with any other area of Atlanta. Two of the more distinctive areas of entertainment were provided to the neighborhood by Walter T. Candler and his brother Asa Candler Jr.

In 1922, Walter Candler led a group of investors in the creation of the Lullwater Driving Club. In spite of being called a "driving club," horse racing was the primary function of the club. The club's first event was held in April of the same year at its racecourse adjourning Walter's home on Lullwater Road. It was a star-studded event attended by many of the South's top opera stars. (Opera performers enjoyed great celebrity at the time among the upper class.)[44] The races were an instant hit, so much so that in 1924 Candler, along with a group called the Presidents Club composed of many of the city's foremost civic leaders, oversaw the completion of a racing plant on Candler's "Lullwater Farm," complete with stables and a track, which, at least in the eyes of journalist George Congdon, "surpasses in beauty Louisville's Churchill Downs."[45] It was within Lullwater Farm where Candler's passion dwelled as he not only bred the horses, but he also often played the role of jockey. Lullwater Farm became a "household name" within the horse racing world by producing top of the line Standardbreds: Lulla Forbes, the Duke of Lullwater and the legendary stallion Abbedale.[46]

While Lullwater Farm must have been quite a sight to behold, one can only imagine the spectacle that must have arisen on April 20, 1932, when an entire express car full of more than thirty wild animals pulled up to the Emory University station. No less awesome a sight, one can be sure, occurred when the animals—among which were a troop of monkeys, two mountain lions, two African lions, a camel, two chimpanzees, two elephants, two Himalayan bears, two leopards, one Himalayan goat, one zebra and two llamas—were loaded onto trucks and delivered to Asa Candler Jr.'s personal zoo, located on his Briarcliff Road estate![47]

Candler began housing exotic animals on his property about a year or so before the 1932 delivery, but on a much smaller scale. Needless to say, the massive addition to his collection, purchased from a European animal dealer based in Nashua, New Hampshire, provided a spectacle the likes of which Druid Hills had never seen.[48] While scores of neighborhood children flocked to the residence in hopes of catching a glimpse of beasts they had only read about, the general reaction by Candler's neighbors was one of shock and outrage.

W.R. McClelland presided over a meeting of the eccentric capitalist's neighbors, and issued the following grievance:

> *Odors from the zoo are terrible at times, particularly when the wind comes our way, although at sometimes they are not noticeable. Roaring of the lions, trumpeting of the elephants, squealing of the monkeys and other animal noises coming from the zoo are annoying and distracting to property owners of the neighborhood; and there is the constant fear and danger that some of the beasts will break out and prowl the vicinity, as has happened.*[49]

The animal escape McClelland was referring to seems ridiculous, even by Hollywood standards. It was his understanding that a monkey escaped from the zoo and accosted a woman on the street, stealing her purse and running up a pole with it.[50] Regardless, one can sympathize with McClelland's complaint. After all, a Druid Hills resident would often complain about the seven-hundred-pound gorilla in his backyard (referring to Emory), to which Candler's neighbors would reply, "Try putting up with two ten-thousand-pound elephants!"

For his part, Candler acted quickly in denying his neighbors' claims of any animals having escaped. He also denied the presence of any unpleasant odors. Another claim levied by his neighbors was that filthy water was draining out of the animals' cages and into the neighborhood, serving as breeding grounds for disease. To that, Candler responded that the zoo had received a perfectly clean bill of health from a DeKalb County sanitary inspector, and he further noted that all waste from the zoo was disposed of through the Druid Hills sewer system and therefore could not be a health hazard. In addition, he reminded critics that the zoo had educational value, as the public could observe animals that most people would never see in person. He also emphasized that many exhibitions would be held at the zoo, with proceeds going to charities such as Scottish Rite Hospital and the Atlanta Humane Society.[51]

Denials were not enough to stop two separate lawsuits from being brought against Candler. One was from McClelland, and the other from Mrs. Mary L. White, who lived across the street from Candler. Both lawsuits—neither of which was successful—were framed around the same grievances: noise annoyance and unsanitary water buildup, along with noxious odors, damage to property value and fear for their well-being in the event of an animal escaping. Mrs. White also claimed as part of her $25,000 lawsuit that one of Candler's baboons—either Amos or Andy, the names given them by Mrs. Candler—escaped one day and attacked her outside her home.[52]

Believe it or not, tales of baboons on the warpath and monkey purse snatchers were not the most bizarre stories surrounding the controversial zoo. In a fiasco that would have been a shoo-in for a "Darwin Award" had they existed at the time, a local dunce named John Lee Butler tried to use the zoo as leverage in an attempt to blackmail Candler. Butler sent him a letter that read:

> *Dear Candler, I need $1,000 for three months for a girl friend who is very sick. I will pay you $500 interest. Keep quiet about this. Leave the money under the last seat on the left on the*

back row of the West End theater. I am not bluffing. If you don't do this I will kill all the
animals in your zoo to show you I am not bluffing. Keep quiet about this thing.

This was the extent of Butler's attempted blackmail. One cannot help but wonder how a man so desperate for money that he resorted to blackmail planned on killing approximately fifty wild animals, including bears, panthers, elephants and eleven lions, all of which would not react favorably when threatened. Even more puzzling is how Butler could actually expect Candler to believe he could pull off such a task. Perhaps he thought that the idea of sneaking onto Candler's property and stabbing the animals to death, or killing them with his bare hands, did not sound too implausible. After all, Butler was financially desperate, so the likelihood of his having the resources necessary to sneak onto the property and kill a small jungle's worth of animals was small. Ludicrous as the threat was, Candler played it safe and informed the police. They, along with postal authorities, followed the directions given by Butler and left a bundle of cash under the seat he specified. When Butler went to carry out the final stage of his master plan, he was apprehended by police and admitted to writing the letter.[53]

When it opened to the public in early September 1932, thousands flocked to the house with a zoo in its front yard. Initial financial results were positive. Admission to the zoo cost thirteen cents for adults and ten cents for children. The money made from admission sales was enough to pay for the zoo's upkeep, food for the animals and employee wages—basically enough to break even, which was fine with Candler since financial gain was not his motivation for creating the zoo. What he would soon find, however, was that the zoo was very much a seasonal business. During summertime, admission proceeds alone were enough to pay for the many expenses that cannot be avoided when running a zoo. However, as the temperature dropped, so did attendance. Unlike running a bar out of one's basement, where one can cut off the electricity if business is slow and not lose money, running a zoo in one's front yard is an endeavor that requires attention 365 days a year. The animals have to eat even if no one is there to watch. Al Langdon, the animal expert in charge of supervising activity around the zoo, estimated that approximately $600 a month was spent on food for the animals. Then there were the water bills (a public pool was created on the property), electric bills, staff salaries and, oftentimes, extensive veterinary bills.[54]

Sporadic attendance numbers and relentless complaints from his neighbors were not the only obstacles Candler faced. In February 1924, the state supreme court ruled that the DeKalb County tax collector, Homer Howard, was within his rights to levy a $100-per-day tax on the zoo, citing a law stating that such a tax could be levied on amusement facilities "in or near a city of more than 50,000 population."[55]

The ruling was another sign that the zoo had to go. In September of the previous year, Candler thanked zoo curator Fletcher Reynolds for a job well done before informing him that he could no longer afford to keep his position. At the same time, the Coca-Cola heir was faced with the question of what he was to do with the animals.[56] Most people have neither the means nor the bravado it takes to keep a lion as a pet, and five-ton elephants are rarely found on a pawnbroker's list of acceptable purchases. The answer came in a fundraising project with the goal of raising enough money to house and care for Candler's collection at Zoo Atlanta in Grant Park. Candler, along with different Atlanta newspapers, sponsored numerous social events to raise money for the improvements necessary to adequately house his exotic beasts. Before the turn of the decade, Candler's animals had found a new home in Grant Park. Though it only lasted a couple of years, Candler's zoo is undoubtedly one of the most fascinating and unique stories found in the history of not only Druid Hills but Atlanta as a whole.

The fact that the Druid Hills site now occupied by Emory's Briarcliff campus was once the home of one of Atlanta's foremost citizens, who happened to have a zoo on his front lawn, has allowed the house to remain on the property, protected as a national historic site. The fact that Candler's neighbors likely began that day in April 1932 like any other, only to return from their daily affairs and learn that the kooky millionaire down the street now had elephants, panthers, lions and tigers in his front lawn just makes the story more endearing.

Chapter 3

Architecture

"Homes Beautiful"

Druid Hills boasts the work of some of America's most prominent architects, one of whom is Lewis Edmund "Buck" Crook Jr. Born in 1898 in Meridian, Mississippi, Buck would move to Atlanta in 1915 to enter the architecture program at Georgia Tech. From there, he entered into an apprenticeship with the firm of Hentz, Reid and Adler. The principal designer of the firm, Neel Reid, took to Buck, and he soon became the firm's chief draftsman. So impressed was Reid with the up-and-coming architect that he brought him along on a "sketching tour" of England, Italy and France from April through July 1922. The "sketching tour" proved especially poignant for Buck four years later when his mentor passed away due to a brain tumor. Reid was only forty. (According to William R. Mitchell Jr., it is important to note that Crook was able to accompany Reid because he was a young man of means. If not for family money, despite all his talent, Crook would not have gone.)[57]

Reid was, along with Hal Hentz, Philip Shutze and Ernest Daniel Ivey, one of Buck's main influences, and his passing saddened Buck deeply. He left an indelible mark on Buck's designs, which Mitchell describes as "traditional in form and usually, but not always, classic in detail; well-planned structures, well-scaled, proportioned, constructed, and sited; delightful buildings of almost all of the many varieties that people needed in the first two-thirds of this century."[58]

In May 1923, Buck left Hentz, Reid and Adler to form a partnership with Ivey. The new firm, Ivey and Crook, quickly aligned itself with Druid Hills, primarily through Asa Candler, a longtime client. One of the firm's first and certainly most recognizable projects was "Lullwater House," built for Walter T. Candler in 1925.

The spacious green park that is now frequented by joggers and families walking their dogs and feeding ducks at the pond was once the hunting grounds of the Cherokee and Creek nations. Settlers took the land from the natives in the 1820s and divided it into land lots. Peter Roadlander and William Pace were winners of the Lullwater area. Quickly, they sold their lots:

This and opposite page: Living at Lullwater House has to be the easiest part of being Emory's president. *Both images courtesy of Rurik Nunan.*

two of the four that make up Lullwater as it is today were sold to Naman Hardman; the other two acres became grounds for a church and cemetery. The church was ultimately destroyed by General Sherman. Before Sherman's march, Dr. Chapman Powell bought a portion of Lullwater in 1840 and then another 180 acres in 1857. In 1863, Washington Jackson Houston bought 600 acres from Powell and began landscaping the grounds, as well as running the mill. Long after Sherman's brush with Druid Hills, Harry J. Carr purchased the old property around Houston's mill with the intent of renovating the mill and building a house (Houston Mill House). The following year, Walter T. Candler bought the remaining 250 acres for his new home.

As became the typical practice of the firm, "Crook made preliminary sketches…and then did much of the actual drafting of the working drawings. E.D. Ivey prepared the specifications, and then acted as the 'clerk of works,' expertly supervising construction that had been drawn and specified."[59] Stone quarried from the area was used to build the house. "Lullwater House" is not only significant for its design (similar to a sixteenth-century English country estate), but also because it established Ivey and Crook, as stated in a 1985 *Emory Magazine* article, as "unofficial architects for Emory."[60] After Lullwater House, the duo replaced Hornbostel as primary architects for Emory University. Their buildings in Druid

Hills range from the high school to the home at 1284 Fairview Road—formerly inhabited by the "real Miss Daisy," Lena Fox.

Crook died in January 1967, just three months after Ivey, ending a partnership that spanned forty-three years, during which time their firm left its emblem on the history of Druid Hills. Crook's mentor, Neel Reid, died at age forty-one. Yet, before his passing Reid had—despite his age—become the foremost residential architect in the rapidly growing "gate city."

Reid was born in 1885 in Jacksonville, Alabama. After moving to Atlanta, his family relocated in 1903 to Macon, Georgia, where Reid apprenticed with Curran Ellis. From there, he and his friend and future partner Hal Hentz moved to New York and attended Columbia University. Reid enrolled in the school's newly created two-year program for students not seeking a degree. During this period, Reid spent a brief time studying abroad at the École des Beaux-Arts in Paris. Following his brief time in New York, Reid moved to Atlanta and joined a partnership with Hentz and G.L. Norrman. Sadly, Norrman committed suicide in 1909. In 1916, Rudolph Adler was brought on as the third partner.

From here, Reid's designs and influence would give rise to what Mitchell dubbed "the Georgia School of Classicists," whose work can be seen in many of the homes on Ponce de

Alumni Memorial Building, Emory University, Georgia

Ivey and Crook constructed Emory's alumni building in 1954. *Courtesy of the Special Collections Department and Archives, Georgia State University Library.*

Leon Avenue and Lullwater, Springdale and Oakdale Roads. Mitchell maintains that "it is no exaggeration to assert that concentrations of designs from Hentz, Reid & Adler...led by Neel Reid, found in these well laid out, tree-shaded green enclaves on the rolling piedmont terrain of North Atlanta, do constitute what Dr. Francis Simkins called 'some of the most beautiful suburbs in all America.'"

Reid's designs became so prevalent within Druid Hills "largely because of his and Hentz's friendship with Frank Adair and Hunter Perry and Forrest and George Adair, all of the Adair Realty Company."[61] The aforementioned is made clear by one of Reid's first jobs in Druid Hills: Frank Adair's home on Ponce de Leon Avenue, completed in 1911. Furthermore, Reid himself lived in two homes on Fairview Road, which showcases ten Reid-designed homes, before relocating to Roswell to pursue other projects.[62]

His last three years were spent primarily bedridden. On Valentine's Day 1926 Reid passed away as the result of a brain tumor. The *Atlanta Constitution* paid tribute to the man who "contributed vastly to the beauty of the city through the fact that he had designed many of the elegant homes, office buildings and other structures, in this city."[63]

Reid designed this "French manor" for Walter Rich, owner of Rich's Department Store, in 1913. *Courtesy of Rurik Nunan.*

Just a few months after serving as a pallbearer in his friend and business partner's funeral, Hentz was welcoming in a new partner, Philip Shutze. Fortunately, he thought of Shutze as "a creative genius of rare endowments."[64] Hentz met Shutze more than a decade earlier while he and Reid were helping to mentor architecture students at Georgia Tech. Reid and Hentz had an immediate impact on Shutze, as Elizabeth Dowling notes in her biography of Shutze: "The example of Reid and Hentz, who had both studied at Columbia University and for a brief period at the École des Beaux-Arts, significantly influenced Shutze's decision to pursue extensive academic training."[65] A prize pupil at Georgia Tech, Shutze was able to follow the path of his Georgia School of Classicist predecessors, and after graduation from Tech he enrolled at Columbia. Upon graduation from Columbia, he continued to follow in the Georgia Classicist line, as he returned to Atlanta to both work for Hentz and Reid and teach at Georgia Tech. These men became synonymous with Georgia architecture, as they helped to start and develop the architecture program at Tech out of their love for architecture. Most of the early classes were taught for free and functioned as forums where the architects could critique one another's work. The reason so many went to Columbia was largely because there was nowhere for them to study in Georgia.[66]

Shutze's career path would take a decided turn from Hentz and Reid's in 1915 when he won the Rome Prize—an architectural design contest worth $3,000, and more importantly, three years of paid travel and study in Italy. The Rome Prize was likely the highest honor

Reid built this house on South Ponce de Leon Avenue for Frank Adair in 1911. *Courtesy of Rurik Nunan.*

"Rainbow Villa," a Shutze home, was commissioned by Asa Candler as a wedding present for his granddaughter. *Courtesy of Rurik Nunan.*

awarded by the American Academy of Architecture that a student architect could receive. Even more impressive, William R. Mead, the academy's president, declared Shutze's submission to be the best student design he had ever seen.[67]

While his teachers at Georgia Tech and Columbia were influenced by the École, Shutze's time in Italy helped generate a preference for the weathered look of the old, Italian stucco buildings. This influence can be seen in "Rainbow Villa," which Shutze designed for Asa Candler's granddaughter (as her wedding present!).

Shutze took Reid's place in what became Hentz, Adler and Shutze. Shutze was the primary designer, Hentz was in charge of business matters and Adler supervised construction.[68] Though Shutze's work is not as prominent as Reid's within Druid Hills, he certainly left his mark. Along with designing houses, Shutze was involved in Emory's development—with designs including the education building, and most prominently, the church school building at Glenn Memorial Church. The church both serves as a Methodist church and an auditorium for Emory's functions, including graduation.

Georgia Tech was somewhat of a Mecca for Georgia Classicists, thanks in large part to Francis Palmer Smith, whose work can also be seen in Druid Hills. Smith graduated from the University of Pennsylvania in 1907, and shortly thereafter, he was chosen to head the new

This 1926 villa holds characteristics no doubt influenced by Shutze's time in Italy. *Courtesy of Rurik Nunan.*

School of Architecture at Georgia Tech. During his tenure, he taught many of Georgia's best young architects, including Shutze and Crook. In 1922, Smith became partners with Robert Smith Pringle. Pringle retired just ten years later, and Smith continued to practice into the early 1960s.[69] Smith designed much of Druid Hills Presbyterian Church, as well as numerous homes within the neighborhood, including the Oakdale Road home of Patillo Lumber Company president John R. Patillo, completed in 1927.

Fortunately, most of Druid Hills' unique homes have been preserved. One of them, Callanwolde, now serves as an arts center, offering classes in literary, visual and performing arts. Concerts and gallery openings are often taking place there, as well as weddings and social events, as many of the rooms are available for rent. Callanwolde was named by Charles Howard Candler in honor of his family's ancestral home, Callan Castle, in Kilkenny, Ireland ("wolde" is an Irish expression meaning "woods"). Hornbostel designed the 27,000-square-foot mansion in a Gothic-Tudor style, and the Candlers lived there until 1959—two years after Charles's death. It was later purchased by the First Christian Church, which subdivided the property, selling four acres on one side and twelve on the other. They also leased the home to an artist, who was intent on using it as an art gallery, during which time the home suffered from considerable damage due to neglect.

The façade of Glenn Memorial Church. *Courtesy of Rurik Nunan.*

This Georgian estate on Oakdale was designed by the founder of Georgia Tech's School of Architecture,

Despite neglect, the First Christian Church was able to sell Callanwolde for $360,000 in 1972. Certain Druid Hills residents—known as the Callanwolde Foundation—led a fundraising campaign that, along with a matching grant from the Open Spaces Program of the Federal Housing and Urban Development Department and a $40,000 grant from DeKalb County, enabled them to purchase the home. In 1973, Callanwolde gained added protection when it was added to the National Register of Historic Places. A decade later, the Callanwolde Foundation accepted responsibility for regulating events, while DeKalb County assumed responsibility for general maintenance.[70]

Druid Hills also boasts homes by W.T. Downing, designer of the Lyndhurst mansion in Chattanooga, Tennessee, and G. Lloyd Preacher, who designed Atlanta City Hall.

The name "Callanwolde" is derived from the family's ancestral home in Kilkenny, Ireland: Callan Castle. "Wolde," an Irish expression meaning "woods," was added to describe Callanwolde's forest surroundings. *Courtesy of Robert Hartle Sr.*

Chapter 4

Good Substantial People in Moderate Circumstances

On a heavily wooded tract of approximately 26 acres lying on the south side of North Decatur Road, about three blocks east of Druid Hills schools and Emory campus, one of the prettiest and quickest home developments has taken place.[71]

The above quote comes from a 1939 *Atlanta Constitution* article describing a new area of Druid Hills known as Emory Grove. The area, located off North Decatur Road and composed of two streets—Westminster Way and Edinburgh Terrace—provides an example of the difference between the "movers and shakers" and the faculty and staff of Emory.

Druid Hills was no longer just a "millionaire colony," but it was now an area shared by middle-class folks looking for affordable, yet aesthetically pleasing homes. Such is what they were given when the two facets of Druid Hills—the millionaires and the academics—merged when Sam Guy, chair of Emory's chemistry department, married into the Candler family. The land on which Emory Grove was built was previously owned by Guy's in-law Asa Candler Jr. Guy realized the need for affordable housing for Emory faculty and staff, and he in turn hired Emory's manager of facilities Neal Smith to build homes for that purpose. Emory Grove, which was placed on the National Register of Historic Places in 2000, was, and still is, an ideal location for Emory faculty and staff, as it is within walking distance of Druid Hills High School, Emory, Emory Presbyterian Church and the Clairmont Road–North Decatur Road shopping center.[72]

Rolling hills were flattened out in the early 1950s for the construction of the North Decatur Shopping Center. While topographically identical today, in the 1950s and '60s it was a weekend hub for teens and young adults to show off their cars or meet up with friends.[73] Stores in this area have struggled to survive throughout the years. WUXTRY Records remains an exception, still hanging around after some twenty-five years—it was once Eric's Beauty Salon. The shopping center's real staple throughout the years is the

L. Neal Smith built and sold many Emory Grove homes. *Courtesy of the Special Collections Department and Archives, Georgia State University Library.*

This and opposite page: North Decatur Shopping Center sits at the corner of North Decatur and Clairmont Roads. The land was once hilly, but it was leveled in the early 1950s for the shopping center's construction. One constant in the North Decatur Shopping Center has been the revolving door of ice cream shops in the building closest to North Decatur Road. *All photos courtesy of the Special Collections Department and Archives, Georgia State University Library.*

steadfast ice cream parlor at the edge of North Decatur Road. Whether Wilson's Ice Cream from the 1950s or Baskin-Robbins' "31 Flavors" from the 1980s and '90s, or whatever it will be called when this is published, there seems some divine force keeping the ice cream makers churning.

The year 1939 was also when the "malling of Atlanta"[74] began with the development of Briarcliff Plaza. Built to serve Druid Hills, Atlanta's first strip mall lies just east of the neighborhood, facing the old Candler Hotel and running parallel to Druid Hills Baptist Church. The intersection of Ponce de Leon and North Highland was suddenly lit by a triangularly shaped neon sign advertising Briarcliff Plaza's centerpiece, the Plaza Theatre. Complimenting the theatre sign were neon signs for Plaza Drugs (no longer exists) and the Majestic Diner.

In the 1970s the Plaza's box office began to advertise for movies like *Swinging Sorority*. The days of *Gone with the Wind* seemed a thing of the past. Drugs and prostitution became commonplace in the parking lot, causing the Plaza Theatre's closing. George LeFont came to the rescue in 1983, purchasing the Plaza, gutting the theatre and returning it to legitimate status. Today, the theatre shows mostly independent movies, and along with the Majestic, it has survived and is now considered a local landmark, largely due to the millions of dollars poured into its renovation under LeFont's period of ownership.[75]

Across Ponce is what used to be the Briarcliff Hotel, where visitors to Druid Hills often stayed. Built in 1925, the building (known as Briarcliff Summit) is now an apartment

Eric's Beauty Salon is now home to one of Atlanta's most popular record stores, WUXTRY Records. This photograph was taken in 1950. *Courtesy of the Special Collections Department and Archives, Georgia State University Library.*

This picture has a big sign near the center that reads "Toco Hill." Toco Hill is another shopping center that emerged during this era. It has since expanded greatly. *Courtesy of the Special Collections Department and Archives, Georgia State University Library.*

complex for many disabled and elderly tenants. Asa Candler hired G.L. Preacher to build the hotel with a specially designed, colorful terra-cotta detailing on the top floor, which Candler used as headquarters for his real estate company.[76]

Many middle-class families, not just those associated with Emory, were purchasing lots in Druid Hills for its value, beauty and location. Such can be seen firsthand in a letter from Oscar, an Atlantic Ice and Coal Company employee, to his sweetheart Ella, describing their soon-to-be home on Cornell Road (which still stands).

Atlantic Ice & Coal Company
Atlanta, Georgia

December 13, 1925

My oh so dear Ella

I have been reading over for the nth time your letter of the sixth and am glad you thought my last letter was the best yet. I am quite sure that you will understand why I can write you that way, before I have finished. It is for no other reason dear little Sweetheart but that I love and love and love you more and more every day and have just got to tell you about it but was afraid was not very successful in trying to do so by letter but just you wait until I see you and then you will understand. I was in hopes and thought would be able to steal away for a day with you before now but so many unexpected things keep coming up to prevent and besides the problems of finding the home has taken a great deal more time than I would have thought possible and simply had to be attended to so as to have it ready for you in time. Am glad to say however that at last one has been found that fulfills most of the conditions I had layed down and have decided to take it. It is a brand new two story house, dutch Colonial style located on Cornell road near Emory University. This is a very desirable locality being in the Druid Hills section but the people are not of the ultra society set just good substantial people in moderate circumstances. The house is about one and a half blocks from the co [illegible] line and there is every convenience such as city water, gas, electric lights etc. and next door neighbor so I don't think you will be lonely in case it should ever happen that no one was there with you. The lot has a frontage of sixty-five ft. and runs back two hundred fifteen ft. The house sits back about fifty feet from the st. There are four bed rooms up stairs one of them however is called a sleeping porch but the only difference I can see is that it has more windows. Downstairs there is a living room, dining room, sun parlor, breakfast room and kitchen and a good large veranda on one side. There are two bathrooms upstairs. All floors are hardwood. The walls are papered in very attractive designs and there is [illegible] also a double garage. In fact it is the best arranged and constructed of the many houses I have inspected and I believe you will like it. I am glad you have decided to stop work on Jan. 1st and know the rest will do you good [illegible] and get just as lazy as you want to but don't forget to write me with lots of [illegible].

Oscar

Many visitors to Druid Hills stayed at Candler's Briarcliff Hotel, now an apartment complex for the disabled. *Courtesy of the Special Collections Department and Archives, Georgia State University Library.*

Across from Druid Hills Baptist Church were the Druid Apartments. In 1928, the *Atlanta Constitution* declared them "among the finest in the city." *Courtesy of the Joe Lee Collection, DeKalb History Center.*

Courtesy of the Joe Lee Collection, DeKalb History Center.

Murder and Mayhem

Druid Hills, like any established neighborhood, has its share of folklore. The *Atlanta Journal-Constitution* commented on this in an article written in 2000: "Druid Hills is filled with stories as intriguing as the network of decaying 'maid walks' that run behind many of its back yards. They include the legend that Al Capone's cronies once holed up there while the gangster was incarcerated at the federal penitentiary."[77] One such story with more documentation involves the 1910 robbery and murder of a streetcar motorman as he came to the conductor's aid.

One April night, conductor William Bryson and motorman S.T. Brown were going about business as usual when they pulled up to the desolate Druid Hills stop, the last on the Ponce de Leon route. According to Bryson, they were making the adjustments on the car for their return trip into town when they were accosted by three black "highwaymen." One of them had a pistol, Bryson said, and the assailant shouted, "Throw up your hands and give us your coin." Bryson obliged and the assailant took his pocketbook and belt containing the company's money. He then allegedly yelled, "Now you turn around and hit the grit!" before shooting the conductor in the back. Prosecutors argued that, hearing the commotion, Brown—who was changing the destination sign on the streetcar—came to investigate, whereupon he was fatally shot in the face.[78]

Bryson then lay clinging to life with no realistic expectation of aid, as the nearest home was a half mile away. Not until the next crew came twenty minutes later and flagged down a passing motorist was Bryson finally taken to the hospital. It was on his testimony, along with the testimony of a woman living with one of the accused, that murder charges were brought against four men: Ed Weaver, Jim Black, Charles Julian and Charles Walker. The woman asserted that all four men arrived at Walker's house, where she was staying. Just minutes earlier she had heard what sounded like gunshots coming from the direction of the streetcar. Furthermore, she testified that the men gave her a pocketbook and ordered her to burn it.[79]

Despite the testimony of two people being the only evidence, charges were quickly brought against all four men, with Walker named as the shooter. "Justice" was swift for Walker, who was tried, convicted and hanged on July 2, 1910. However, a few months later Bryson admitted that, since he did not actually see Brown get shot, Julian could have been the shooter. Bryson claimed to remember Julian standing over him with the pocketbook and then walking through the streetcar. Within what he considers a sufficient amount of time to walk to the front of the car, Bryson says he heard the shot that killed his partner.[80]

In 1911, after being sentenced to hang, Weaver swore to the court that Julian and Black, who were still in prison, were innocent and were not in fact at the robbery. The *Atlanta Constitution* concluded that "indications are…that the man who committed the actual murder in this case, the slayer of the motorman, is the only one to make a getaway, for having once been in jeopardy, he cannot again be tried."[81] The man they are describing is Emmet Walker, another defendant, who was exonerated by Bryson's inability to place him at the scene. In retrospect, the case seems to exemplify people's shock and horror at this brutal crime occurring in the "millionaire colony"—how the crime occurred was not as important as having someone to blame.

This crime was so brazen that it sent a collective shiver up the spines of all Druid Hills residents. The fact that it occurred within the neighborhood was shocking, yet the victims were not residents of Druid Hills. The most shocking and fascinating crime in Druid Hills occurred in the fall of 1943 with the murder of a resident—not just any Druid Hills resident, but a Candler. Though he was not a blood relative of the man who founded the Druid Hills Company, prominent banker Henry Heinz had married Asa Candler's daughter Lucy Elizabeth.

In 1943, Druid Hills was being prowled by a burglar, and residents were on edge. According to Lucy, she and her husband were relaxing in their library on the evening of September 29 before the 10:00 p.m. radio news broadcast, when they heard noises coming from the left wing of their home. Lucy did not want Henry to investigate out of concern for his safety, and she convinced him accordingly. After growing tired, she went upstairs and showered before going to bed. Upon stepping out of the shower, Lucy was startled to hear her husband's voice screaming, "Mama, Mama, that devil is in here. Get the gun quick!" Lucy did not have to think; she knew "that devil" was the burglar. Before calling the police, she called their neighbor Dr. Bryant K. Vann, who rushed over to the home, gun in hand.

Around the same time, Atlanta Police Officers Marion Blackwell and Bill Miller, assigned to patrol the area, received a call reporting a burglary at 1610 Ponce de Leon. Upon arriving at the scene, Miller found a disheveled Lucy, who claimed the burglar was still inside. As

Miller went inside to investigate, his partner was shining the patrol car's headlights on the back of the house. As Blackwell stepped out of the car into the pitch-black night, he heard gunshots and quickly realized they were aimed at him. He alerted Miller, who rushed outside and joined in the ensuing gunfight. At one point, just as two officers arrived as backup, Blackwell pointed his gun at his assailant's face and pulled the trigger. Blackwell's conscience was spared a beating when all that happened, according to author Bruce L. Jordan, was that "the gun made a fizzling sound and the lead bullet simply rolled out of the barrel." As you probably guessed, this was a good thing because the man at whom he was firing was, in fact, Dr. Vann. Both Blackwell and Vann thought, in the dark of night, that the other was the burglar. Blackwell was the better shot, however, and he put bullets in Vann's shoulder and chest, neither of which proved fatal. Before this fiasco, Miller had found an obviously deceased Henry Heinz lying in a pool of his own blood inside the home.[82]

Not surprisingly, panic ensued throughout the city in response to the murder of one of Atlanta's most prominent citizens in his exclusive Druid Hills estate. What followed was the largest manhunt in Georgia's history. As Jordan notes, with any high-profile case, the longer the search for the perpetrator continued, the more widespread and ridiculous the conspiracy theories became. The Heinz murder was no exception, with lingering post-Depression resentment toward the rich contributing heavily to rumors that Vann and Lucy were in cahoots to murder Heinz for his money.[83]

About a year and a half later, on January 14, 1945, police officers stopped a black man driving a blue car with no headlights. Upon inspection, they found the man, who told them he was a railroad worker on his way home when his lights went out, to be sober and let him go with a warning. However, they did take down his license plate number. Later that evening, the wife of a prominent Atlanta attorney entered her bedroom only to find a large black man rummaging through her closet. Upon finding her pocketbook, he ran out of the house to a blue car. He left behind a blue bandana, which the police found on the driveway. Police were able to link the bandana to a six-foot-three, 230-pound black man named Horace Blalock. Surprisingly, he had no prints on file, but he confessed to fourteen burglaries in the North Atlanta area.

Police were then able to compare his fingerprints with an unidentified set found at the Heinz home the night of the murder. The results: a perfect match. Confronted with the evidence, Blalock, who police found to be very amiable, originally confessed only to burglary, but after some time he admitted to fatally shooting Heinz. Even after his trial and conviction, rumors continued to swirl about a possible coverup. As Jordan notes, the home became a topic of folklore: "After the murder of Henry Heinz, the Heinz mansion was rumored to be haunted. Occupants reported hearing gunshots in the night and believed the mansion was being haunted by Henry Heinz. The mansion fell into disrepair and became an overgrown monument to the tragedy."[84]

Chapter 5

Creating Cultural Community

Churches, Schools and Fernbank Museum

Churches

Glenn Memorial Church is one of two types of churches within Druid Hills, one that was built as a church and not converted from a house. It was designed by Hentz, Adler and Shutze, who drew acclaim for their mastery in creating what looks like a colonial-style church, yet can also function as an auditorium.

The church came about as a result of the ever-growing faculty and staff working at Emory who wanted a Methodist congregation in Druid Hills. In 1920, a meeting was held to oversee the organization of the Emory University Methodist Church, led by seventy-three charter members. It was soon decided that the church would be named for the Reverend Wilbur Fisk Glenn, who had been a fixture of leadership in the Southern Methodist Church for fifty years prior. The church's principal donors were his children, Thomas K. Glenn and Flora Glenn Candler, wife of Charles Howard Candler Sr.

The church opened in 1931 to the delight of Flora Glenn Candler, the church's prime benefactor over the years. In 1940, she floated the bill for the new church school building, which is highlighted by Shutze's "Little Chapel," fashioned after St. Stephen's Walbrook in London. To this day, the church remains a sanctuary for worship and a magnificent auditorium for many Emory events.[85]

Druid Hills Baptist Church is another landmark for the neighborhood. Completed in 1928, the Southern Ferro Concrete Company built Druid Hills Baptist in the Italian Renaissance style. It flourished in a time when religion was as much a part of Atlanta life as five o'clock traffic is today. Every Sunday, the sanctuary was packed elbow to elbow—a stark contrast to the attendance numbers now. You can attend Sunday services and not see but one or two children in the half-full sanctuary, whereas in the church's early days Sunday school attendance was record breaking. The July 1930 issue of the *Sunday School Builder*, a

Parishioners of Druid Hills Baptist Church could walk next door and eat brunch at the Charles Restaurant or The Seminole Grill. *Courtesy of the Special Collections Department and Archives, Georgia State University Library.*

publication that was solely devoted to covering Sunday school news throughout the country (also indicative of how different 2008 is from 1930), praised the church for its exponential growth. The numbers it reported are almost unbelievable, especially compared with today. In 1925, when Dr. Joseph Broughton took over as Druid Hills Baptist's superintendant of Sunday school, there were already about 500 Sunday school attendees per week. Four years later, the average weekly attendance was tabulated at 1,558 people.[86]

Such a turnout could be largely attributed to the head pastor, Louie D. Newton. Since 1919, Newton was copastor with the church's original voice, F.C. McConnell. Armed with the gift of gab, Newton remained at the pulpit until 1968. To his congregation, Newton was a truly magnanimous figure. Senior adult coordinator and unofficial church historian Martha Manning fondly recalls the days of her youth when Newton's radio broadcasts and *Christian Index Weekly* articles were the talk around the dinner table. She recalls Martha Berry, of Berry College, and "anybody who was anybody—judges, lawyers, doctors, from Druid Hills"—crowding the church on Sunday and nodding approvingly at Dr. Newton's sermons. Nowadays, she says, the church is fighting an uphill battle just to get young people to show up to church-sponsored events. Despite waning attendance, the church remains a sight to

A 1956 aerial view of Druid Hills Methodist Church. *Courtesy of the Special Collections Department and Archives, Georgia State University Library.*

behold—from the massive columns outside to the orb-shaped designs in the woodwork surrounding the baptistery—as well as a link to Druid Hills' golden age.[87]

Druid Hills Methodist Church also accommodated many of the neighborhood's favorite names, including Judge John S. Candler, who once owned the property on which the church now stands, and E.D. Ivey, who, along with his partner Crook, designed the church, which opened in December of 1953. Located at 1200 Ponce de Leon Avenue, the church has made numerous renovations over the years, including refurbishing one of the finest pipe organs in the state.

At 1428 Ponce de Leon stands one of Druid Hills' most unique and eye-catching homes. The light yellow brick building surrounded by white marble columns is now known as Saint John's Melkite Church. Melkite Catholic origins lie in the Middle East, so the home, which looks like an Arabian palace, was ideal for the congregation to hold Mass when they bought it from the American Legion in 1955. The American Legion had owned the building since 1946, when they bought it with the intent of making it their headquarters as well as a war memorial. From 1943–1946, the home was a boardinghouse for fifteen tenants. Before that, the home had remained closed for over a decade.

A postcard depiction of Candler's Ponce de Leon palace, drawn when it was still residential. *Courtesy of the Joe Lee Collection, DeKalb History Center.*

The Candler mansion, with an unkempt lawn in the early 1950s. *Courtesy of the Special Collections Department and Archives, Georgia State University Library.*

The church paid just $62,000 for the building, a far cry from the $210,000 originally paid by Asa Candler in 1916. Candler built the home for his wife, Lucy Elizabeth Howard, who intended for it to be a party house. Upstairs was decorated lavishly with regal furniture and stained glass imported from Europe. The highlight is a thirty-five- by sixty-five-foot sunken atrium with a pink marble mosaic floor. A lavishly decorated dining room and music room was often filled with the Candler's adult guests, while downstairs the children enjoyed a massive game room, which included a bowling alley.

Unfortunately, Mrs. Candler never saw the home's full fruition as she passed away in 1919, with furniture still on order from Europe. (The home did play host to famous guests including evangelist Billy Sunday and President Taft.) Candler lived in the house after Lucy's death. In 1923 he remarried, and his new wife, her sister and her twin daughters all gladly moved in. In 1926, Candler took ill and spent most of his last three years in a hospital bed. Upon his death, his wife and her family moved out and the house closed. Today, the Melkite church has preserved the original design as much as possible, making only the necessary changes to create a church-like setting. They often open their doors during the Druid Hills Tour of Homes.

Saint John's Lutheran Church shares more with Saint John's Melkite than a namesake. Both are converted from the mansions once owned by some of Druid Hills' elite. Edward Dougherty's design was completed in 1914 for Sam H. Venable, who, along with his brother, was one of the largest operators of the stone quarries in Stone Mountain. The house embodied the spirit of Druid Hills at the time, as it was built from only the finest granite from Stone Mountain, which Venable had been collecting for a quarter century. Venable built it with the intent of providing "hospitality and good-living for all of [his] friends."[88]

Now, the mansion serves as part of Atlanta's oldest Lutheran church, Saint John's. Organized in 1869, the church was located first on Marietta Street and then in Inman Park before moving to its current home at 1410 Ponce de Leon Avenue. About $60,000 was all the church paid for the gothic mansion designed in the Tudor style. They bought it in 1959, and then invested another $50,000 to turn it into a church. In 1969, the firm of Baker and Cunningham's sanctuary design was completed, built from the same type of granite as the original house.

Preston Arkwright was the former proprietor of what became the Jackson Hills Baptist Church in 1955. That year, the church purchased twelve acres on South Ponce de Leon Avenue with the intention of relocating from its building on Boulevard and Rankin Street. The site included the former Georgia Power Company president's Swiss Tudor–style home named "Pinebloom." According to a 1973 *Atlanta Journal* article, "it was named for the old Colquitt place in Albany [GA]." So the legend goes when the pollen fell and it was a deep gold it signified richness in the nation. In other words, the pollen really bloomed. The blooms, then combined with the pine trees, resulted in the name, "Pinebloom."[89]

Originally, the church intended on demolishing the Druid Hills staple, but it decided instead to build its sanctuary in limestone casting adjoining the home. The rooms were converted to fit the parish's needs—for example, the former living room became a small chapel. However, as attendance waned when many of the former parishioners found new

Choir practice at Jackson Hill Baptist. *Courtesy of the Vanishing Georgia Collection, Georgia Division of Archives and History.*

churches to avoid making the drive to Druid Hills, so did the building. Deterioration of Pinebloom's ceiling even forced services to be held in the basement in 1983. Now the building is in much better repair after hundreds of thousands of dollars were put into restoration.[90]

In 1989, Pinebloom served as the temporary home for Atlanta's Quakers while they searched for a new place of worship following the sale of their meetinghouse at 1384 Fairview Road. It was surprising to learn that they had too many members to continue to hold services at the Tudor home, which had been built in 1926 for a family with Quaker ties. In 1959, the Atlanta Quakers bought the home and remained there for thirty years. The Society of Friends left an interesting history in Druid Hills—just a year after buying the home, the Quakers welcomed Dr. Martin Luther King Jr. for a seminar on nonviolence. Dr. King was giving the seminar in preparation for Atlanta's public school integration, which was an issue of deep concern for the Quakers. They also held meetings for black and white students and their families, as well as protests against the Vietnam War and some of the first integrated classes.[91]

While the Quakers were peacefully protesting, another religious group was packing up its tambourines and getting ready to plant its roots in Atlanta. Hare Krishna was born in 1966. The religious group was founded by Srila Prabhupada and was popular within the "hippie movement." Hare Krishnas, or members of the International Society of Krishna Consciousness, seek to achieve a higher state of consciousness, by following many Hindu principles. The name "Hare Krishna" was given to the sixteen-word chant (mantra) that followers believe eases stress and other worldly interruptions and, by doing so, creates a "pure" consciousness. Typically, they are known for their saffron robes, sandals, shaved heads and tendency toward chanting in public. Yet today, Krishnas are encouraged to build stable homes and families, hold stable jobs and help maintain the temple.[92] The Atlanta temple is inside a home on South Ponce de Leon and was named New Panihati Dham by Prabhupada when he visited Atlanta in 1975.

Atlanta Krishnas visited the village Panihati Dham, India, in 1976, to attend the famous Panihati festival. Ever since then, they have staged their own festival in tribute. Krishnas from all around, as well as plenty of curious locals, can be seen munching on "chopped rice," a crispy rice and yogurt dish that has become a staple at the festival.[93]

Druid Hills Golf Club

No high-end neighborhood is complete without some sort of golf or country club. Druid Hills Golf Club celebrated its opening in late April 1914 at an event described by the *Atlanta Constitution* as follows:

> *Despite the clouds that came and went in the morning, the sunshine stayed, and made it possible for the Druid Hills Golf Club to entertain four hundred guests as much al fresco fashion as inside. Even before the hour of the reception at 4 o'clock there had assembled on*

Druid Hills Golf Club, Atlanta, Ga.

A 1919 postcard depicting the entranceway to Druid Hills Golf Club. *Courtesy of the Vanishing Georgia Collection, Georgia Division of Archives and History.*

the terraces many bright parties of people, who marveled at the picturesque setting of the clubhouse; the beauty of the blooming dogwood blossoms and the green of the terraced grounds as far as the eye could reach.[94]

The Druid Hills Golf Club was chartered on September 24, 1912, after a petition for use of approximately a hundred acres was submitted to the Fulton County Superior Court by the Druid Hills Company—specifically, by J. Carroll Payne, Lowry Arnold and I.A. Hammond.[95] The course was designed by H.H. Barker. It immediately became one of Atlanta's premier social and recreational hotspots, frequented by the likes of Georgia Power President Harry Atkinson, Coca-Cola owner Ernest Woodruff and, of course, the Adairs. Days at the club were spent playing golf or tennis and enjoying tea in the clubhouse, while at night, Japanese lanterns hanging from trees illuminated dances and other social functions. "Gastronomic Zazas" was how Paul Warwick described the club's barbecues, attended by "lovely ladies, fortunate men, and happy celebrities."[96] These were opera stars, the "movie stars" of the time, such as Jeanne Gordon and Jose Mardones. Even President Warren Harding and the first lady enjoyed lunch at the club in 1921.

Numerous golf tournaments have been held at the club throughout the years, the most notable being the Dogwood Invitational Tournament, which ran from 1941 to 1972 and was reinstated in 1994.

Fernbank Museum

The sixty-five-acre area known as Fernbank Forest was once the roaming grounds for the Creek Indians. Today, Fernbank Museum describes the woodland as "the largest old-growth urban Piedmont forest in the country."[97] Sometime between the time of the Creek Indians and today, the forest served as the playground for a young girl named Emily Harrison. In 1938, upon retiring from teaching, Harrison enrolled at the University of Georgia to study her true passion—forestry. Apparently, her study evoked many pleasant memories of her youth, which she spent playing among the trees and brush, as she made preservation of forests her goal.

Harrison, along with her friend Dr. Woolford Baker, chartered Fernbank Inc., which purchased the forest and named it for a creek bank within the forest that was covered by ferns, of which she was especially fond.[98] With the advent of Fernbank School, Fernbank Inc. formed a partnership with the DeKalb County school system, allowing for instructors to use the forest to teach biological sciences and requiring that the county create a conservation and management program as means of added preservation. The partnership continued to grow, and in 1964 the Fernbank trustees donated four acres to the county for the creation of Fernbank Science Center, which celebrated its ribbon- cutting in 1967.

By the late 1970s, Fernbank trustees had their collective eye on expanding the center into something bigger, something the public could enjoy. Local philanthropists such as Rankin Smith, who was the original owner of the Atlanta Falcons, jump-started fundraising for a massive, 160,000-square-foot museum. Graham Gund architects got to work on the project in 1989 and completed it in 1992. That same year, on October 5, the museum opened its doors to throngs of eager patrons. Reaction was mostly favorable. An *Atlanta Journal-Constitution* headline read: "Problems with parking and complaints about over-sophistication clouded a few impressions, but most everyone found something to praise at the new Fernbank Museum of Natural History when it opened Monday."[99]

In 1993, the museum's first full year of operation, attendance hit 542,407. However, largely because of the complaint that there was a lot of museum space and few exhibits to fill it, attendance numbers started to dwindle. Things got so bad that in 1996, after the museum could not pay its bills, a "consortium of banks and the Woodruff Foundation came to the rescue."[100]

The museum has since expanded its collection so that visitors no longer feel as if they have received a 6-foot-tall, gift-wrapped present with nothing but a thimble inside. In 2001, it opened its most impressive exhibit to date, the Giants of the Mesozoic. The exhibit is jaw-dropping, featuring a 123-foot-long skeletal reconstruction—the largest of its kind in the world—of the *Argentinosaurus* (just about the only thing that could make the 86-foot-tall atrium look full). In the exhibit, a flock of pterosaurs and other prehistoric animals provide the background for a hypothetical battle between the *Argentinosaurus* and another carnivorous giant, the *Gigantosaurus*. The exhibit alone is worth the price of admission.

The Saint Catherine's Island Foundation and Edward John Noble Foundation Collection was added in 2004. While not as awe-inspiring as the Giants exhibit, the exhibit—resulting from thirty years of research by Dr. David Hurst Thomas, curator of North American archaeology at the American Museum of Natural History—provides a truly fascinating view into Georgia's history. Most significantly, the collection provides detail into the history of a Spanish mission colony that existed on the barrier island of Saint Catherine from the 1570s to approximately 1680—over fifty years before Oglethorpe founded Georgia as a colony. The exhibit also provides insight into prehistoric human activity on the island, ranging as far back as five thousand years ago.

The museum has become a welcomed addition to the spacious piedmont forest.

Schools

The need for primary education in Druid Hills became a topic of concern when Emory moved in. With the influx of faculty also came their children. While there were schools such as Antoinette Johnson's kindergarten, elementary and high schools were not readily available. As a result, the Emory Grammar School emerged. Located on Emory's campus, the school was privately funded and, in 1925, employed eleven teachers who were responsible for seven elementary and three high school grades. The graduating sixth-grade class of 1922 marked an annual addition of grades until 1927, when the first class was graduated from high school. By this time, it was clear that with the expansion of both Emory and Druid Hills as a whole, a new campus was necessary.

Druid Hills' residents and Emory faculty signed a petition asking for the creation of a Druid Hills school district and for the issuance of building bonds for a new school. In May 1927, the board of education approved the creation of a Druid Hills school district, with W.D. Thompson, Walter T. Candler and Fred C. Mason elected trustees for three, two and one year(s) respectively. The Trust Company of Georgia posted the highest bid for the $250,000 bond, and Ivey and Crook were employed to design the school. After surveying a few sites around the neighborhood, the firm decided on the ten-acre plot where the school sits today. It was purchased from Emory University for $10,000. Shortly thereafter, Harry J. Carr was chosen to construct Ivey and Crook's plans. Less than a year later, in April of 1929, the building was completed.[101]

Druid Hills School was composed of kindergarten through eleventh grade until 1952, when its school board became part of the Dekalb County school system and, as a result, added a twelfth grade. Richard Sams recalled, in a presentation for his 1956 class reunion, two turning points for the school brought on by the 1960s: "First, Druid Hills, like all Southern schools, became racially integrated, and second, the 'postwar Baby Boomers' became high school age. As a consequence, Druid Hills High soon became overcrowded with more than 1,800 students in grades 8–12 alone."[102] Consequently, two new elementary schools—Fernbank and Shamrock—were formed, and Druid Hills housed only grades eight through twelve.

The 1970s brought an increased budget as well as the "M to M" (Minority to Majority) busing program. The following decade saw an increase of special needs programs such as special education and learning disability units. The year 1987 marked the incorporation of Briarcliff High School into Druid Hills High. Both schools were marked with decade-long fledgling attendance, with more and more parents enrolling their children in private schools. As a result, the school board voted six to one in favor of making 1986–87 the last school year at Briarcliff High.[103] Ten years later, Shamrock High School met a similar fate when it became solely a middle school, sending its graduates to Druid Hills, which now had only grades nine through twelve. In 1997 Druid Hills became the first charter school in Dekalb County. This title afforded it "the autonomy to implement teaching strategies that improve student achievement."[104] The charter ended in 2002 and was not renewed. However, in 2004, Druid Hills was approved for the International Baccalaureate Degree.

In 1971 a new school emerged in Druid Hills with a heavy focus on the arts. A group of six parents, concerned that the public school's art programs were inadequate, decided to form a school of their own. With the advice of Elliot Galloway, founder of the Galloway School near Buckhead, the parents leased the former home of Arthur Harris at 1341 Ponce de Leon Avenue.[105] The Reid-designed home, built in 1912, was transformed into a school with an initial enrollment of 140 students. In 1973, the school purchased the adjoining property in order to make room for a high school. Expansion continued throughout the 1980s, including the construction of a new gym and theatre complex, which opened in 1989. The year 1995 saw the opening of a 25,000-square-foot high school building. Under the direction of Paul Bianchi, Paideia's first and only headmaster, the school has grown to

Local students outside of Druid Hills High School. *Courtesy of Robert Hartle Sr.*

an annual enrollment of about 900 students and has earned a reputation as one of Atlanta's finest private schools.[106]

Driving Miss Daisy

At a July 6, 1910 meeting of Druid Hills stockholders, a resolution, which stated that "no offer on any lot in Druid Hills shall be refused solely on the ground that the prospective purchaser is a Jew,"[107] was adopted.

Nowadays, such a statement would be considered inane, but at the turn of the twentieth century, nondiscrimination was not a given. Anti-Semitism was strong throughout the country, and it directed its spotlight on Georgia during the 1913 trial of American Jew Leo Frank. Frank, a Texas native, moved to Atlanta after graduation from Cornell University and found work managing a pencil factory. On April 27, 1913, the body of Mary Phagan, a thirteen-year-old white factory worker, was found by the night watchman at the factory. Amidst much controversy and racial strife, Frank was convicted of murder. Originally sentenced to death, Frank's sentence was changed to life in prison after evidence used against him came into question. However, in 1915, an angry mob calling itself "the Knights of Mary Phagan" kidnapped and lynched him. This sparked racial tensions in Atlanta, leading to a revitalization of the Ku Klux Klan and the formation of the Anti-Defamation League. Decades later, the Frank story was the basis of the Alfred Uhry musical *Parade*.

Uhry is Druid Hills' biggest celebrity. Born and raised in Druid Hills, Uhry grew up in a wealthy family of German-Jewish heritage during a time when subtlety was necessary when it came to practicing the Jewish faith in order to be accepted within the community. Before matriculating at Brown University, the playwright joked, "I didn't know how to pronounce schmuck."[108] This relationship between Jews and the rest of Druid Hills helped inspire one of the masterpieces of American cinema, *Driving Miss Daisy*.

Uhry, a 1954 graduate of Druid Hills High School, first earned recognition when he helped turn Eudora Welty's *The Robber Bridegroom* into a musical. His efforts helped the musical win a Tony Award, but it was with *Daisy*—the first of his "Atlanta Trilogy" (the second was called *The Last Night of Ballyhoo* and the third was *Parade*)—that Uhry received worldwide acclaim. The play opened in New York in 1987 and was eventually adapted, by Uhry, into an Academy Award–winning film (Best Picture and Best Screenplay) starring Jessica Tandy, Morgan Freeman and Dan Aykroyd.

The script centers around an elderly Jewish woman named Daisy (Tandy) living in 1950s Atlanta. She is no longer able to drive and, at the insistence of her son (Aykroyd), she hires a black chauffeur (Freeman). Initially, Daisy, a cranky woman, seemingly set in her ways and not open to change, refuses the services of Hoke, her new chauffeur. Yet after time, Hoke accomplishes what not even her son is able to do—he brings joy to the old woman's life. Their resulting friendship captivated critics and audiences and brought a sudden wave of attention to Druid Hills.

It was this redbrick home on Lullwater Road that provided the setting for the critically acclaimed *Driving Miss Daisy. Courtesy of Rurik Nunan.*

Alfred Uhry chose this house, which reminded him of his grandmother, on whom the character Daisy is based. *Courtesy of Rurik Nunan.*

Much of the filming was done at 822 Lullwater Road. The character Daisy was based primarily on Uhry's grandmother, Lena Fox, and "Hoke" was based on his grandmother's chauffeur, Will Coleman. The red brick, Tudor home provided the ideal setting for a film that, to this day, ranks as one of the top American films of all time.

The Druid Hills Home and Garden tour had always been a favorite among locals. However, in 1990, after the release of *Daisy*, the tour, which showcases an annual array of Druid Hills' finest and most original homes, including 822 Lullwater, drew approximately four thousand visitors—double the previous year's total.[109]

Uhry also helped write the 1988 screen adaptation of the play *Mystic Pizza*, which starred Julia Roberts. In 1999, he was honored at Druid Hills High School in what could be called a "roast." The school organized a fundraiser for renovations to what became known as the Alfred Uhry Theatre. All of this was to the delight of the man who practiced his love of theatre at Druid Hills High, writing, among other things, a musical, which he recalled as "something godawful about a cruise to Paris and Pompeii and all these places I'd never been."[110]

Chapter 6

Emory International

Over the past few months, I have discovered a pattern that occurs when I tell one or more people about this book. They will most certainly ask, "How did you decide to write about Druid Hills?" And, if there is more than one member of the inquisition, someone will invariably jump to my defense with "The Central Park guy!" or "Olmsted designed it!" (To tell you the truth, before I started on this project I had no idea who Frederick Law Olmsted was. Furthermore, I had no idea that so many people knew who Olmsted was.) This is where I take issue: granted, it is quite exciting to be able to tell people that the man who laid out the original plans for your neighborhood is the same man who designed Central Park, but Olmsted should not be the name synonymous with Druid Hills. If there is one name that should be synonymous with Druid Hills, it is Candler. Besides purchasing the land and development rights to Druid Hills from a then financially depleted Joel Hurt, Candler was the driving force behind the move that has shaped Druid Hills' development for the last eighty-odd years—the founding of Emory University's Atlanta campus.

Asa Candler was born in 1851 in Villa Rica, Georgia. Though his father was a successful merchant and planter, Candler was far from a spoiled child as he was one of eleven children growing up in a strict Methodist household. Rather than remaining in Villa Rica, at the age of twenty-one Candler packed up his belongings and moved east to Atlanta. Intent on entering the pharmaceutical business, Candler spent his first day in Atlanta applying for jobs. One job was at the Pemberton-Pulliam Drug Company. Though he did not get the job, Candler would later become a business associate of "Doc" Pemberton, the company's president. After becoming a prosperous pharmacist himself, Candler returned to the Pemberton-Pulliam Drug Company with a reported $2,300, enough to buy the patent, equipment and recipe for Coca-Cola. We all know how that turned out.

Two major factors contributed to Candler's decision to throw his financial weight behind Emory's Atlanta campus. The first is fairly self-explanatory: Asa's brother, Bishop Warren

Asa Candler (second from left) poses with his family in the late nineteenth century. *Courtesy of the Vanishing Georgia Collection, Georgia Division of Archives and History.*

Candler—originally reluctant, but later overwhelmed by a sense of providence—became president of Emory College, in 1888.

Providence, at least in Candler's mind, was the only explanation for the second factor. In the early twentieth century, Vanderbilt University was the South's home for Methodist higher education. No one was more determined to see this relationship continue than Warren, whose opinions on matters of spirituality Asa held in the highest esteem.

However, after his dismissal from Vanderbilt's board of education in 1905, Warren saw the board, especially University Chancellor James Kirkland, as both a thorn in his side and a mounting disgrace to the Methodist Church. He was alarmed that, despite being owned by the Methodist Church, Vanderbilt's faculty was primarily non-Methodist and, in 1905, employed only one Methodist dean out of seven.

The rift worsened when steel tycoon Andrew Carnegie arrived on the scene. Carnegie was far from a religious man, adhering more to the progressive social ideals of the day. Carnegie was also convinced that secular education was the only proper form. Philanthropically speaking, he had interesting motivations, one of which was distaste for the poor wages paid to professors. As a result, he established a $10 million pension for retired professors, provided they came from secular universities. Carnegie continued his not-so-subtle attack on religious-based education when he offered Vanderbilt University a total of a million dollars in donations, provided their endowment board became secular.

As Mark Bauman noted, Warren Candler was, in many respects, a typical Reconstruction-era Southerner. He saw the Carnegies and Rockefellers of the North as subversives, intent on destroying Southern culture—within which the presence of God was essential in all aspects—and replacing it with a culture intent on measuring "intellectual attainments…by ounces or pint cups."[111] Fearing that such a subversive element would be chomping at the bit to poison what remained of nonsecular education, Warren reminded his fellow bishops that:

> *If from the work of education, by which modern life has been enlightened and elevated, the contributions made directly and indirectly by the Church were subtracted, the remainder would be an inconsiderable residuum.*[112]

This was the last straw for Warren Candler and his fellow Methodist bishops. Infuriated, they demanded that the school refuse Carnegie's donation. When their demands were not met, the General Conference of the Methodist Episcopal Church, South, gathering in Oklahoma City, voted to sever ties with Vanderbilt University.

Just like that, the forty-year relationship between Vanderbilt and the Methodist Church came to an end. Not one to rest on its laurels, the church quickly announced plans for two new Methodist universities, one on each side of the Mississippi River. Dallas, Texas, was chosen as the site for the western university, and construction on Southern Methodist University was soon underway.

The location for the eastern school was narrowed down to either Atlanta or Birmingham, Alabama. Only one of these premier Southern cities was called home by a devout Methodist with a million dollars burning a hole in his pocket. On June 17, 1914, Candler penned what is now known as his "million-dollar letter." Candler's letter to the educational commission of the Methodist Church promised a million-dollar donation for the establishment of a university east of the Mississippi River, dedicated to "the advancement of sound learning and pure religion."

The "million-dollar letter" never makes any sort of stipulation that the university must be built in Atlanta. However, Candler tactfully and subtly implies as much at the letter's end:

> *In humble trust in the Christ to whom I look for salvation, I dedicate the means with which Providence has blessed me to the upbuilding of the divine kingdom. In the confidence that my brethren and fellow citizens of Atlanta, of Georgia and of our Southern Methodist connection will join with the Commission in carrying this great enterprise to speedy and large success, I offer this contribution to its foundation.*

The educational commission took the hint, and within just three months classes had begun in Emory's first academic department—appropriately enough—the School of Theology.

By the time of his death in 1929, Candler had donated some $8 million to Emory. The university charter holds that "the Methodist Episcopal Church, South, is and shall be always regarded and held to be the founder of the University." However, if one looks in Emory's administration building, one can find a plaque dedicated to Asa Candler with the inscription: "Founder of Emory University."

Candler's influence on Emory was not limited to his wallet. For example, Henry Hornbostel of Palmer, Hornbostel and Jones was chosen to develop Emory's campus plan. The actual building of the campus—which Alistair Cooke, during a BBC broadcast, called "the most beautiful in America"[113]—was awarded to Arthur Tufts, an architect out of Baltimore, Maryland. Coincidentally, both men were previously commissioned by Coca-Cola. (Ivey and Crook would take over as primary builders after building "Lullwater House.")

Hornbostel immediately took notice of the similarities between this area of Atlanta and his favorite part of the world, Northern Italy. The "rolling hills and pines" would, he proposed, be complemented nicely by an Italian Renaissance–style campus, built primarily with marble. Candler agreed and a plan was expeditiously drafted, enthusiastically accepted by the building committee and put into the works.[114]

Tufts dove headfirst into the development project, and by 1917, he had overseen the building of the theology and law schools, Winship and Dobbs Halls (dormitories), John P. Scott Laboratory of Anatomy and the T.T. Fishburne Laboratory of Physiology. Two years later, the physics building and a third dormitory, Alabama, were erected, thus completing the first stage of development.

By 1919, amidst this rapid development, Warren Candler felt that he had given all he could as Emory's president. A search began for a suitable replacement—an educated Methodist man, with the energy and ability to unite the different schools into one cohesive university. They found such a man in former University of Florida philosophy professor and

Construction of the Emory Law School building nears completion. *Courtesy of the Vanishing Georgia Collection, Georgia Division of Archives and History.*

Southeastern district supervisor of the Student Army Training Corps—now the ROTC—Harvey Warren Cox.

Cox learned almost immediately the importance of appeasing Asa Candler. Within four years of his inauguration, Cox had made significant strides in doing so by ordering each school to balance its own budget and putting a hold on any further development until fiscal matters were resolved. So impressed was Candler by Cox's fortitude and resolve that he gave to Emory what is every university's favorite two gifts: land and money, a million dollars and fifty-five acres, to be exact.

Drawing his attention away from the budget, Cox threw himself into academics. One order of business was restructuring Emory's undergraduate curriculum. A "lower division," which provided for a very broad education during freshman and sophomore years, and an "upper division," which provided for an intensely specialized education during junior and senior years, were created. Cox also oversaw the creation of a new two-year junior college in Valdosta, Georgia, and the transformation of Emory University Academy from a prep school into another two-year junior college. All three campuses featured the same "lower division" curriculum in an effort to make easier the transition to the Druid Hills campus.

After balancing the budget and restructuring the curriculum, Cox and the board of trustees met in June of 1925 to discuss fundraising. At the time, Emory's endowment totaled slightly more than $2.5 million, a number not even close to the endowments held by the country's top universities (Harvard, Yale, etc.). Cox realized that, to be mentioned in the same breath as these elite institutions, far more resources were needed. As a result, the self-explanatory "Ten Million in Ten Years" plan was initiated, allotting $7 million to the endowment and the remainder to building construction.

Initial results were promising as the university raised $750,000 within the plan's first year. Despite the plan's initial success, times were about to get tough, not only for Cox, but for the university as a whole. The Great Depression hit in 1929 and paid no mind to sectional differences. Both the North and South were hit with unprecedented financial decline. Emory University was no exception. Enrollment dropped, the budget was drastically reduced and all plans for expansion were put on hold indefinitely.

The leadership qualities responsible for Cox's hiring were now being put to the ultimate test. The university's very future was now in question, and Cox would have to make some of the most difficult decisions of his life. Normally a stoic, Cox could no longer hide his emotions at a faculty meeting during which he announced that faculty salaries had to be cut. Goodrich C. White, then dean of Emory College, recounts with great admiration how Cox handled the matter:

> *The only time I ever saw him* [Cox] *give way to feeling was when he had to announce* [at a meeting of the faculty] *the imminent necessity of a salary cut, and the faculty had responded with a spontaneous expression of loyalty and confidence. He broke down then; and for some minutes he could not speak. The faculty whose interests were so deeply his had shown that they believed in and trusted him. That broke him, where difficulties and problems never*

could. In every crisis, great or small, his poise [was] *unshaken, his courage undaunted, his decision unfailing.*[115]

The faculty's trust and loyalty to their president was made clear when chemistry professor J. Sam Guy—notorious for his opposition against administrative intrusion—proposed the vote of full confidence in President Cox. Only one faculty member opposed the vote, proving that, from top to bottom, Emory faculty believed that Cox was the man to lead them through these tough times. Ultimately, the faculty's faith in their president was rewarded. The year 1934 saw the second faculty pay cut, reducing salaries by 15 to 21 percent. However, the following year saw a 5 percent salary raise and, by 1937, a full salary restoration was completed.[116]

By 1941, President Cox was wearing down. Declining health led him to announce his retirement, effective at the close of the 1941–42 academic year. His goal of finishing the academic year as president could not be achieved as his health worsened. His longtime friend and admirer Goodrich White was named his successor. After stepping down as president, Cox accepted the position of chancellor, which allowed him, sans administrative responsibilities, to remain involved with the university, primarily through public relations.

Emory University's first president died on July 27, 1944, leaving behind a legacy that reads almost like a handbook for university presidents. His devotion to the university was matched only by his levelheaded management of academics and finances, exemplified in his leadership throughout the Great Depression.

It is not difficult to understand why Cox chose Goodrich White as his successor. An "Emory man" if ever there was one, the devout Methodist was graduated from Emory College in 1889 at the age of eighteen. From 1914 to 1918, White taught psychology at Emory College, until he was made a lieutenant in the psychology division of the Army Medical Corps. After receiving his doctorate from the University of Chicago in 1927, he moved to Atlanta and was soon appointed dean of Emory College. From 1938 to 1942, White served alongside Cox as his vice-president.

White's term as president lasted from 1944 to 1957, the last eleven years of which would see Emory's campus nearly double in size. Enrollment also increased dramatically, but in a more frenetic manner. During his first few years as president, White was overseeing an enrollment that hovered around fifteen hundred students total. Clearly—as White was well aware—this number would jump fairly significantly when World War II ended. What he could not have predicted was that, come 1947, there would be roughly seven hundred more servicemen in residence at Emory than there were total students in 1938.

To accommodate this influx of new students, University Treasurer George Mew purchased over a hundred war surplus trailers. The trailers were placed between Winship Hall and Clifton Road and, along with thirty-one prefab buildings, were used to house the bulk of married students and their families. Approximately 672 single male students were placed in either one of three federal public housing dormitories or in one of two officers' quarters inside Chamblee's Naval Air Station.

ROTC students stand at attention in front of McTyeire Hall in 1944. *Courtesy of the Special Collections Department and Archives, Georgia State University Library.*

The arrival of new students certainly warranted the appointment of new faculty. Again, the same problem arose: Where would they live? In response, White successfully petitioned the board of trustees to allow for the building or purchase of 114 faculty housing units along Haygood Drive and North Decatur Road. (Ironically, now Emory is buying back these houses, often at much higher than market value, as part of a development project involving Emory Hospital.)

By the early 1950s, White had successfully guided Emory through its post–World War II transition, and he was ready to start building. In 1951 alone, Emory added an unprecedented ten new buildings, including the history building, Beta Theta Pi and Tau Epsilon Phi—the first two houses on Fraternity Row—the Woodruff Memorial Building and the administration building. White's most prolific developmental undertaking was the building of the Clifton Road Emory Clinic, completed in 1956. A group of seventeen physicians, who four years earlier began a private practice under the dean of the medical school devoted to treating patients on campus while allotting at least a fourth of their time to research and instruction, were the first of a rapidly increasing number of physicians to practice at the clinic.

Another difficult issue placed before White was that of coeducation. Nominally, Emory was a male-only university; however, certain exceptions were made for numerous women

A picture from the early development period on Haygood Drive. *Courtesy of the Special Collections Department and Archives, Georgia State University Library.*

Excavations begin for the building of Emory Hospital. *Courtesy of the Vanishing Georgia Collection, Georgia Division of Archives and History.*

Emory Hospital as it looked during the 1950s. *Courtesy of the Special Collections Department and Archives, Georgia State University Library.*

throughout the years. Still, there was nothing in the charter that addressed this issue. What did exist was a formal agreement between Emory and Agnes Scott (an all-female college) acknowledging that Emory and Agnes Scott were not in competition with one another and, therefore, Emory would not admit female students. After it became clear that Agnes Scott College would not oppose rescinding the agreement, a board meeting was called and a vote was taken allowing Emory to become a coeducational institution.

However, as Gary S. Hauk notes, it was no coincidence that Emory fully opened its doors to the fairer sex about one year into the Korean War. After all, President White had only to look back seven-odd years to recall how World War II had sapped Emory's enrollment. Further enrollment-control tactics were implemented, including establishing a unit of the Air Force Reserve Officers Training Corps on campus. In the fall of 1951, after being chosen as one of sixty-two colleges to administer these training corps, both Emory College and the School of Business Administration began courses on air science and tactics. As a result, the Atlanta campus had 285 new students, while the Oxford and Valdosta campuses added 461 between them.

When he announced his retirement in 1957, Goodrich White had earned a reputation as a masterful fundraiser, having raised Emory's assets from about $20 million at the time of his inauguration to $52.5 million, $28 million of which was endowment. Equally important,

Emory's Class of 1945 files into the auditorium in Glenn Memorial Church. *Courtesy of the Special Collections Department and Archives, Georgia State University Library.*

as we have already discussed, was his success in maintaining stability within the university in the face of World War II and the Korean War. Finally, as Thomas H. English asserts, White helped put Emory on the national stage through two personal achievements: in 1946, White was chosen by President Truman to serve on the President's Commission on Higher Education and, in 1952, he became the first Southerner elected president of the United Chapters of Phi Beta Kappa.[117]

Emory's next five years would be guided by former University of Georgia dean of arts and sciences Dr. Sydney Walter Martin. Martin, like his predecessor, owed much of the credit for his appointment to their mutual friend, chairman of the board Charles Howard Candler. (As a sidenote, it is by no means my intent to make this seem like some sort of sleazy "I scratch your back, you scratch mine" appointment. Candler admired these men based on their merit and conviction, but without his respect, there is little doubt that neither would have been elected.) Sadly, just two months into the Martin presidency, Charles Howard Candler passed away.

Yet, even from beyond the grave, it appeared as if Candler was still looking out for his appointee. Subsequent to Charles's death, his widow Flora Glenn Candler offered the family mansion, "Callanwolde," to the university. After deliberation between Mrs. Candler and the university, it was agreed that her generous offer was better suited for another recipient (unspecified). Philanthropy proved to be a quality shared by both husband and wife when the widow Candler offered Emory an endowment gift equivalent to "Callanwolde's" value. Emory did not find this offer better suited for another recipient. They graciously accepted, and in 1959 the Charles Howard Candler Professorship was created. Since its creation, the Candler Professorship has been awarded to some of the nation's preeminent scholars. Current Charles Howard Candler Professor of Philosophy Donald P. Verene comments on its significance:

> *I remember as an undergraduate, I met (Philosophy Professor) Charles Hartshorne and he was a Charles Howard Candler Professor. Hartshorne was then and still is, considered one of the most important philosophers of the twentieth century. I never imagined I would have the same Professorship as him.*

In 2007, there were about thirty Charles Howard Candler Professorships in various departments.

Emory's purchase of Walter Candler's "Lullwater House" in 1958 provided what would become the home to future presidents and their families. The 185-acre estate, which still stands, has been the home to every Emory president since Martin. Most of the land was converted into "Lullwater Park," a beautiful example of the rolling hills and massive oaks that make Druid Hills so alluring.

Development continued under Martin as a result of a growing student body, which now included a substantial number of women. Three new female dormitories—Hopkins, Smith and Thomas Halls—were occupied in 1958. Other developments included Harvey W. Cox Hall (opened in 1960), which provided new food services on campus, and the renovation of Dobbs and Winship Halls.

Unlike White, Martin never knew the difficulty of presiding over Emory during a foreign war. However, Martin did have to deal with a war at home—the war between the federal government and the government of Georgia over the issue of segregation. According to Hauk, Martin "provided little leadership on the issue."

The landmark Supreme Court decision in *Brown v. Board of Education* (1954) reversed the ruling of the court in *Cumming v. Richmond County Board of Education* (1899)—the case that validated the ruling in *Plessy v. Ferguson* (1896), which sanctioned the constitutionality of segregation in public schools. Nowadays, it is difficult to imagine the chaos that this ruling must have caused. Aside from the issue of whether African Americans belonged in the same schools as whites, the ruling provided the federal government with the right to demand that states integrate schools.

Georgia Governor S. Ernest Vandiver and the state legislature fervently opposed integration and threatened to shut down the entire public school system if the court mandated integration. In the second ruling of *Brown v. Board*, the court ruled that the district courts of each state would be responsible for school integration, to be carried out "with all deliberate speed." To reiterate, it is impossible for someone who was not alive at the time to fathom the tension and widespread controversy that must have occurred. In fact, I am inclined, out of my own ignorance, to picture a room full of politicians, sweating profusely and gnawing on their collars, waiting on pins and needles for their district court to order school integration, whereupon the governor would pull some giant lever that would shut down all public schools.

What actually happened was slightly more reasonable. In January 1961, Federal Judge William A. Bootle ruled in favor of two African American students, who were refused admission to the University of Georgia. The pair was suing on grounds that UGA had denied their admission for no reason other than race. Judge Bootle concurred, and UGA was ordered to admit Charlayne Hunter and Hamilton Holmes Jr. Governor Vandiver now had the unenviable choice of either obeying the federal government or following Georgia law, which demanded that all funding be cut for any school that integrates. Because he had promised his constituency during his gubernatorial campaign that he would follow this law, it is plain to see why Vandiver originally ordered UGA to shut its doors. Yet, because he was a politician, it is just as plain to see why the man who once called the *Brown v. Board of Education* ruling a "judicial monstrosity" quickly changed his mind when confronted with the reality of crossing the federal government. The governor called a special session of the state legislature and pled his case for repealing antidesegregation laws. The legislature backed him and the laws were repealed.[118]

Georgia legislature's compliance with federal law actually made Emory's decision regarding integration more difficult. Georgia law stipulated that private educational institutions must remain segregated in order to claim tax exemption. Initially, the university's stance was that, as soon as tax laws made it possible, it would accept qualified African American students. Words turned to action in 1962 after an African American applied to the Dental School. The university filed a "Petition for Declaratory Judgement and Injunction," asking the court(s) to determine whether Emory would be allowed to integrate African Americans without losing its tax-exempt status.

Henry L. Bowden, Emory's chairman of the board, and Ben F. Johnson, the law school dean, were charged with preparing the case. To make a long story short: after losing in the lower courts, Bowden and Johnson successfully appealed to the Georgia Supreme Court, which ultimately ruled that private schools would be allowed to admit any qualified applicant, regardless of race, while maintaining tax-exempt status.

Bowden, along with Chancellor Goodrich White and dean of the faculties Judson Ward, was chosen to form a triumvirate that would run the university after President Martin relinquished his duties in June of 1962. This was a temporary solution until a suitable replacement could be found. In July of 1963, after a lengthy courtship by Bowden, former Cornell University provost Sanford Soverhill Atwood was named Emory's next president. Despite having to address a budget deficit and an "inadequate endowment," Atwood was determined to put Emory on the national stage. He was not going to attempt this from the comforts of his office either. Rather, for the first year of his presidency, his life was more akin to a politician on the campaign trail than a university president. Much of his first ten months as president was spent traveling and giving speeches in an effort to mingle with various alumni and other possible benefactors. Apparently pleased with the results, Atwood set in motion his MERIT (Mobilizing Educational Resources and Ideas for Tomorrow) program, selecting banker and Emory trustee William Bowdoin as chairman. MERIT, initiated in 1965, aimed to raise $25 million in four years. When the four-year timetable expired, MERIT had raised $10 million more than its original goal, making it the most successful fundraising effort in Georgia's history.

During his seventeen-year run as president, Atwood was nothing less than a fundraising machine. His retirement in 1977 culminated in a stretch that saw $150 million worth of construction, including the Robert W. Woodruff Library, the Dental School building and the Nell Hodgson Woodruff School of Nursing, to name a few projects. Furthermore, Atwood's presidency saw the number of faculty double and the student body increase by over 60 percent.

James T. Laney was promoted from dean of the Candler School of Theology to Emory's next president in 1977. Like Atwood, Laney envisioned Emory on a grand stage. In 1979, Emory's executive committee initiated a new fundraising campaign, dubbed "the Campaign for Emory." Unbeknownst to Laney—a Yale graduate and former Methodist missionary— his prayers were about to be answered by a college dropout turned car salesman.

George Woodruff convinced his brother Robert to make the largest monetary donation to a university in American history, not because of the originality of the slogan "the Campaign for Emory," but as a result of new legislation, which made the fund started by their parents a taxable entity. The aforementioned fund was named the Emily and Ernest Woodruff Fund after Robert and George's parents. This new legislation demanded that they give away all of the fund's income, or 5 percent of its assets, whichever totaled more. The Woodruff brothers reorganized the foundation into a "supporting organization," which was tax-exempt, provided all income went to a set group of recipients. Robert Woodruff was nearly ninety years old when he gave "the Gift": approximately $105 million, which was composed primarily of Coca-Cola stock that had grown exponentially over the years.

Emory's greatest benefactor was a child of means, born in Columbus, Georgia, in 1889. In 1893, Robert and the family moved to Atlanta when his father took a job working under Joel Hurt at the Atlanta Consolidated Street Railway Company (became Georgia Power Company). About a decade later, his father would become president of the Trust Company of Georgia (became SunTrust).

Apparently, Robert and his father were very similar. In December of 1908, after one dismal semester at Emory (Oxford), Robert agreed with President James Dickey that he should take the spring semester off. After holding a few jobs here and there, he landed a job as a salesman with the Cleveland, Ohio–based White Motor Company. From the get-go, Robert's sales record was astonishing and, by 1921, he had earned a place on the company board. Woodruff's success was duly noted by his father Ernest, who had recently led a conglomerate of businessmen in the purchase of the Coca-Cola Company for $25 million in 1919.

The Coca-Cola Company got off to a sluggish start, partly as a result of inflated sugar prices post–World War I. Steady leadership was critical at this point, and Ernest Woodruff could think of no better leader than his charismatic, business-savvy son. After some cajoling, Robert begrudgingly accepted the position as president of the Coca-Cola Company. Ironically enough, the president of the company that produces what is now the most popular soft drink in the world took a $50,000 a year pay cut from his job at White Motor Company to lead Coca-Cola. There is no need to go into specifics concerning Coca-Cola's fiscal achievements. Suffice it to say, Robert made a wise decision by accepting the pay cut.

Through aggressive domestic and international marketing and increased bottling, Woodruff transformed Coca-Cola from a local success to an international phenomenon. Woodruff cannot be described as a man with so much money he didn't know what to do with it. Yes, he was "rolling in it," but as someone with the discipline and leadership to head a company on the global stage, such as Coca-Cola, he knew how to disburse his riches and he knew where he wanted them to go.

On the surface, Woodruff's donating such colossal amounts of money to Emory seems about as likely as Bill Gates giving a couple billion dollars to the bully who made a practice of holding his head in the toilet every day. It is clear that he was miserable at Emory, so why didn't Robert rub his success in the university's face? There are a few answers. First of all, he simply was not that kind of person. Second, a relationship between Coca-Cola and Emory already existed from the Candler days. Finally, after visiting his Ichauway Plantation in Baker County, Georgia, Woodruff became appalled at both the physical devastation induced by malaria on many of his workers and the resulting economic malaise. As a result, Woodruff recruited various faculty from Emory's School of Medicine to treat his workers and to collect data on malaria.[119]

Robert was impressed with the results, and his interest in public healthcare continued to grow, especially when his mother passed away from cancer in 1937. That same year, Robert donated the funds for the creation of the Winship Cancer Center, which opened in 1939 and was named for his maternal grandfather.

Emory deserves its share of credit for Woodruff's philanthropy; that is, Woodruff was not going to give his money away randomly. He had to trust the judgment of those he entrusted with his finances. Thanks to the successful management of the money he allotted for these first few projects, Woodruff would form a philanthropical bond with Emory, giving some $230 million during his lifetime. (Robert's brother George Woodruff, who had an equal say in the Woodruff Fund, helped convince Robert that Emory was right for "the Gift" because it would best manage the fund.)[120] Six different buildings on campus are named for, or were named by, Robert: the Robert W. Woodruff Library; the Nell Hodgson Woodruff School of Nursing (named for his wife); the George W. Woodruff Physical Education Center; the George and Irene Woodruff Residential Center (for his brother and his wife); the Woodruff Memorial Research Building (in honor of his father); and the Robert W. Woodruff Health Sciences Center Administration Building.[121]

By the time he stepped down as president in 1993, Laney had achieved more than anyone could have hoped for, largely thanks to the Woodruff Fund. He succeeded in providing more scholarships (such as the Robert W. Woodruff scholarship created in 1981) to attract top-tier students; in creating new facilities and renovating old ones (the George W. Woodruff

Physical Education Center and the Pollard Turman Residential Center, both opened in 1983, and the George and Irene Woodruff Residential Center, just to name a few) in order to attract new students and improve the quality of life for existing students; and in placing Emory on the national stage through efforts such as recruiting speakers like acclaimed Irish poet Seamus Heaney and former Russian President Mikhail Gorbachev.

Emory's eighteenth president, William Chase, had landed a pretty good gig when he assumed responsibility in July 1994. Emory was recognized as one of the premier universities in the country, and it boasted an endowment ranking in the top ten in the nation. Chase would continue expanding the campus, investing roughly $1 billion in numerous renovations and new facilities. Emory's research funding grew by about 65 percent and, from 1996 to 2000, the School of Medicine had a faster growth rate in research funding than any other school in the country. Emory's sixty-four-acre residential complex, dubbed the Clairmont Campus, was erected in 2003 and houses about fifteen hundred students. Emory had first planned to build a performing arts center during the Cox era, but it was unable to do so as a result of the Great Depression. Finally, in 2003, three-quarters of a century later, the Marvin Schwartz Center for the Arts was built at the intersection of Clifton and North Decatur Roads.

Today the university is presided over by biomedical engineer James W. Wagner and continues to flourish. In 2005, Emory drew worldwide headlines after selling the rights to Emvitra—the leading anti-HIV drug—which was developed by Emory Professors Dennis Liotta and Raymond Schinazi, along with researcher Woo-Baeg Choi. The university continues to attract some of the biggest names in both academia and world affairs. In 2007, the Dalai Lama, leader of the Tibetan exile community, accepted a university appointment for the first time when he was named presidential distinguished professor at Emory.[122]

Emory continues to grow. As anyone who has even passed through Druid Hills recently can attest, the soothing sounds of tractors and jackhammers fill the air of much of the neighborhood. With seemingly never-ending development, it appears that the "700 pound gorilla" in Druid Hills' backyard is getting fatter and fatter.

Emory and Druid Hills have been intertwined since the Methodist Church, South, selected Atlanta as the site for its eastern university. Emory's influence is not only seen through building, but through people and cultures as well. I would argue that Emory has made Druid Hills a microcosm of Atlanta. Atlanta's population explosion in the 1990s brought an influx of residents to the city who moved here from all parts of the country and the world. Emory, in large part due to its commitment to affirmative action, a diverse student body and a diverse range of study, has also attracted people of all races, geographic locations, et cetera, into its educational melting pot. (Driving in Druid Hills, I have become a master of state license plates. I recently saw my first Alaska plate, and need only to see a Hawaii plate to make it to all fifty).

In August of 2006, the *Atlanta Journal-Constitution* announced the hiring of Bryan Cooke as executive director of its new Clifton Community Partnership. Cooke, who completed his MBA at Emory's Goizueta Business School and lives in a Mediterranean villa in Druid Hills designed by James Lawrence Turner in 1925,[123] was put in charge of the program with a mission statement that reads:

The Clifton Community Partnership (CCP) is an initiative started by Emory to provide a framework for local residents, employers, employees, businesses and local governments to work together to foster a healthy living-learning-working environment and to improve the quality of life throughout the Clifton community. The term "Clifton community" is defined by the CCP as the three-mile radius surrounding the heart of Emory's campus.

CDC

One of my most vivid memories from adolescence stems from the release of the 1995 film *Outbreak*. While my friends were thinking about the Braves winning the World Series and the upcoming Summer Olympics, I was huddled in my room, covered in a blanket of paranoia, trying to come to grips with the fact that all of the flesh-eating, face-melting diseases on the planet were just a five-minute walk away. Every time I passed the CDC (Centers for Disease Control and Prevention) I pictured the look on Kevin Spacey's face when his protective suit ripped open and he was infected with the "Outbreak" virus. Every morning I expected to step outside and see—rather than my smiling neighbors walking their dogs, or bringing their kids to school—a group of pockmarked, pus-oozing mutants, stumbling awkwardly with outstretched arms, trying to infect as many people as possible before their heads fell off.

Twelve years later, I must admit, I sometimes pass by the CDC headquarters and get the shivers. During my research of the CDC, I came across some recent information that provides an example of the pendulum on which the CDC has swung. Combing through recent *Atlanta Journal-Constitution* articles, I came across one dated December 1, 2007, that reported that the CDC had detected a new strain of the Ebola virus. Granted, this is nothing to jump for joy about, but I felt a sense of security that they had identified the strain and can hopefully control it before it can migrate from Uganda. Despite the presence of a flesh-eating disease nesting up the road at the CDC headquarters, I not only was glad it had been identified, but I also took solace in the fact that the CDC had, over the past few years, greatly increased security. However, as I started perusing the articles, in order of most to least recent, my sense of security was short-lived.

Within minutes, I came across another article that appeared intriguing. Skimming over it, I first glanced at a line that read: "The outage shut down air pressure systems designed to contain deadly germs for about 60 minutes. No injuries were reported."[124] Though I was happy that no injuries were reported, I couldn't help but flash back to Kevin Spacey in *Outbreak*—except now, the lights had cut off and a bunch of doctors in white coats were flailing about as clouds of disease circled their heads. My delusions were temporarily lifted, until I recalled another article I had passed over. It was dated August 16, and the headline was nearly enough to compel me to leap under my desk: "Crews Blasting 30 Feet From Deadly CDC Germs." The article recounted that, on May 18, 2007, a construction crew that was blasting rock had accidentally shattered three lab windows and damaged another two. One of the broken windows happened to be on the same floor as the Ebola virus.[125] Again, no injuries were reported.

Besides scaring the life out of me, these three articles typify the history of the CDC since its inception: it has alternately been lauded for its success in containing one disease and criticized for not identifying another. Basically, the CDC has many of the most important jobs on earth. While a police detective is showered in praise (and rightfully so) upon apprehending a serial murderer, the detective likely spent many a sleepless night wondering when the killer would strike again. Now, imagine a CDC doctor in charge of stopping the spread of SARS or anthrax. The staff at 1600 Clifton Road have been placed in these positions and will continue to be. Naturally, these top doctors will be successful in some endeavors, and not in others. But, no matter what, these endeavors, often with global consequences, will occur in Druid Hills, a neighborhood known for rolling hills and classic houses, not SARS and anthrax.

CDC first stood for Communicable Disease Center when it was formed in 1946. That same year, under the direction of Public Health Service leader Dr. Joseph Mountin, it arose from the agency that had been called the Malaria Control in War Areas (MCWA). Malaria had proved an efficient killer of U.S. troops in World War I and continued to be a major source of concern for decades, especially in Georgia. Prominent Druid Hills resident Preston Arkwright, along with his stepson, Emory physician Dr. Glenville Giddings—who likely played a major role in Woodruff's interest in public health—were among those leading the fight against the spread of malaria. Under the leadership of Dr. Mountin, and ultimately decided by Surgeon General Thomas Parran, Atlanta was chosen as the site of MCWA's headquarters.[126]

In 1947, Woodruff donated the land on Clifton Road where the CDC now stands. However, the headquarters was not dedicated until thirteen years later. Despite success in the 1950s— such as helping to remedy the "Cutter incident" when poliomyelitis contaminated the Salk vaccine, which was given to children to prevent the virus—funding for the Druid Hills' building was hard to come by. Elizabeth W. Etheridge suggests that an increased emphasis on medical research provided the reason for groups such as the National Institutes of Health to be funded generously, while the CDC remained in "makeshift shelters contrived from barracks, hospital wards, mess halls, and portable buildings."[127]

In 1955, the House and the Senate both approved an appropriation of $12,330,000 for construction of a new headquarters, yet delays continued when, in 1957, President Eisenhower deferred construction on government buildings. That same year, a Democratic representative from Rhode Island named John E. Fogarty became a top lobbyist for the CDC when he testified before the House Subcommittee on Appropriations on the CDC's deplorable working conditions, which he had observed during a recent visit to the Chamblee branch.

While Fogarty lobbied in the House, Democratic Senator Lester Hill of Alabama lobbied in the Senate. These two, along with Surgeon General Leonard A. Scheele, composed the CDC's lobbyists in Washington. After years of delays, these advocates proved vital in the eventual completion of the new headquarters at 1600 Clifton Road. In fact, Fogarty was the speaker at the September 8, 1960 dedication.

When operations got underway at the new building, it was decided that the Montgomery, Alabama branch would close—much to the chagrin of Senator Hill—in addition to the

Chamblee branch. However, while transferring the organisms held in these buildings lacked the humor that had been present when trucks full of giraffes and apes barrelled down Briarcliff en route to the Candler Zoo, there was no lack of danger present. After all, it is not as if these samples could simply be boxed up and thrown in the mail, or tossed in a plastic bag and thrown in the garbage. The problem with moving the specimens was that they were kept in freezers at a temperature of seventy degrees below zero. After a few days opining over what to do, Jim Paine and his staff came up with the answer: they placed bags filled with wet sawdust into every opening between the specimens. Then, the freezer door was taped shut and left that way for two days. Finally, on midnight of the second day—so as to travel at the coolest time of day—the freezers were hauled into trucks, driven to Atlanta and plugged in at the new headquarters.

Since then, Druid Hills has been at the epicenter of global health issues. One of the first would prove to be among the greatest victories for world health in history: the eradication of smallpox. In 1962, the disease, which had existed for thousands of years but had become almost obsolete within America, surfaced in a Canadian boy who had recently traveled through a New York airport. This prompted the CDC to create a smallpox surveillance unit, led by Dr. Donald J. Millar. The unit, which also included Doctors John Neff, Ronald Roberto, Thomas Mack and J. Michael Lane, not only studied how smallpox arrived in countries, but also influenced one of the key developments in smallpox vaccination. They suggested that Defense Department employee Aaron Ismach develop a vaccine injector that was not dependent on electricity. The result was named the "Ped-o-Jet." It was powered by a foot pedal and capable of administering up to a thousand injections within an hour. Best of all, it could be used in countries where smallpox was most prevalent, namely countries where electricity was not readily available.

Initial tests on the machine were fruitful, yet little attention was paid in America as the disease was not a common threat. Not until D.H. Henderson suggested that smallpox eradication be included with an existing program, that of combatting measles in Africa, did eradication efforts begin. Henderson had studied the current program for measles vaccination and had found it deficient insofar as it reached only one-fourth of African children. He believed that, because approximately a thousand people could be vaccinated against smallpox for the price of one measles vaccination, a joint measles-smallpox eradication program was only logical. Apparently, Henderson was convincing as he received support from President Johnson, whose plan was for smallpox to be completely eradicated by 1975.

With the president's support, the CDC drafted a five-year plan for dual vaccination in West Africa. Henderson was chosen to lead the new Smallpox-Eradication Program (SEP), charged with the CDC's role in the eradication of smallpox in West and Central Africa. The United States' concern with smallpox prompted a minor increase in funds allocated by the World Health Organization (WHO), yet as Etheridge suggests, the "lack of enthusiasm may have stemmed from the failure to eradicate diseases in the past. Beginning with the campaign against hookworm in the American South in 1906…and including the global efforts against yellow fever and malaria, the concept of eradication had everywhere failed."[128]

Preston Arkwright (left) not only played a major role in the origins of the CDC, but also in the origins of Druid Hills as a whole. *Courtesy of the Special Collections Department and Archives, Georgia State University Library.*

Granted, the newest staple in Druid Hills had a lot on its plate, but it definitely had the right man for the job. Henderson knew, while others did not, that surveillance would be the ultimate key to eradication. Different plans were developed for different countries, taking into account political landscape, economic stability, et cetera, and numerous teams of doctors and other medical professionals were assembled in Druid Hills. Before any of the teams shipped out, they were faced with a change in command when Henderson was named head of the WHO's smallpox-eradication program.

Now under the direction of Millar, teams headed for Nigeria and Sierra Leone, where they quickly realized that the WHO's estimates of smallpox cases in the area were much too low. Undeterred, the teams battled hostile residents, miserable living conditions and warring tribes, and still were able to celebrate their hundred-millionth vaccination in 1969.

A few years prior, Henderson's ideas on surveillance were implemented by, among others, Dr. William Foege when an outbreak occurred in the small town of Ogoja, Nigeria. A lack of supplies forced Foege and his fellow doctors to decide, through surveillance and containment, which of the exposed should receive vaccination. By the time further supplies arrived, the smallpox was gone.

Besides the obvious—fewer vaccines equals less money spent—there were cases in which people died from being vaccinated. Foege therefore created a three-group system of surveillance data in order to identify "those that required no special attention; those that required consultation to improve surveillance but not an all-out drive; and those like Togo and northern Nigeria that required supplements of equipment and personnel." This process was implemented in Sierra Leone, where, after a nine-month stretch in which less than 70 percent of the country's population was vaccinated, the virus was obsolete.[129]

In 1973, Foege, now heading the CDC's smallpox effort, moved his family to India where he would share his expertise in eradicating smallpox. There, he implemented his system effectively again. If a case of smallpox was reported, a containment team went to the village in which it was reported. From there, they confirmed the case, vaccinated all residents and identified the source of the infection. Guards were then placed around the homes of any victims. When most of the containment team left, a few would stay behind to vaccinate new residents.

By 1978, after the CDC processed over four thousand specimens taken from various countries throughout the world and found them all negative for smallpox, the WHO could officially say that smallpox had been eradicated.[130] It was one of the greatest achievements in healthcare history, and more than some of it occurred in this small Northeast Atlanta neighborhood.

Three years later, a call came in to the CDC from two concerned doctors in Los Angeles. Dr. Michael Gottlieb, along with Epidemic Intelligence Service (EIS) officer Dr. Wayne Shendera, was treating five young men, all of whom had been previously in good health, for a very rare form of pneumonia. The only sort of link the CDC could establish between the men was that they were all "active" homosexuals. In July 1981, twenty-six cases of Kaposi's sarcoma—a form of cancer almost exclusively found in elderly men—were reported among homosexual men living in New York and California.

The fact that these cases were so unlikely was made even stranger by the proximity in time during which they occurred. Additionally, as Elizabeth W. Etheridge states in *Sentinel for Health*:

> *The addition of a third factor—the appearance of the diseases in a particular segment of the population—was a fire bell in the night. It meant one of two things: there was a very high attack in a localized area, or the problem was relatively common and only the tip of the iceberg could be seen. From the very first, they were afraid it was the second possibility.*

The original name given to the disease was KSOI (Kaposi's sarcoma and Opportunistic Infections). Dr. James Curran, along with Dr. Harold Jaffe and Mary Guinan, was charged with heading an informal task force on the puzzling new illness. Quickly, they would realize that it would not simply die out. By this time, the number of cases was doubling every six months and, due to the lack of specific conditions associated with KSOI, the CDC found itself baffled. All that was apparent was that it was arising in, almost without exception, homosexual men, who, upon contracting it, could not fight off infection. The disease was a death sentence and it was only getting stronger. "So many more would die. But even before those first cases were reported, we knew the problem was sufficiently serious," lamented Curran.[131]

Surveillance again was key. Jaffe and Guinan were sent to San Francisco to compare homosexual men with KSOI to homosexual men without the disease. What they found was a difference between the healthy men and the infected men insofar as the infected men had significantly more sexual partners than the healthy men, who generally had only one partner. This prompted further investigation, this time by Dr. William Darrow, the CDC's senior sociologist. Darrow, along with another doctor, was able to track down as many names as possible of former sexual partners for thirteen of the first nineteen KSOI patients. From this information, Darrow was able to link forty current KSOI patients in ten different cities. It was becoming clear that the disease could be transmitted sexually.

News continued to worsen when the disease claimed the lives of three hemophiliacs. An inquiry was done, and it was determined that the only way these three could have been infected was through tainted blood from a transfusion. Immediately, Curran called a meeting with government and special-interest groups to discuss the burgeoning disease. Two things occurred in the meeting: one, the name AIDS was established; and two, the KSOI task force began preaching caution as an essential means of AIDS prevention. Curran urged listeners—to no avail—to discourage possible carriers from donating to the blood bank. Curran saw this mid-1982 meeting as the start of what he called the "year of denial," during which many gay groups were concerned with AIDS being labeled a "gay disease," while many hemophiliacs still refused to believe the disease was bloodborne. It was not until the summer of 1983, after exponentially increasing numbers of the aforementioned groups, as well as exponentially increasing numbers in places such as Haiti and Zaire, had been infected, that the world began to fear what Curran and his task force had feared since first encountering the disease.

In short, as Etheridge describes it, panic ensued overnight:

> *The public's and, to an extent, the government's discovery of AIDS came in mid 1983. Public demonstrations protested the government's lack of action in dealing with the epidemic, the dilemma of those with AIDS being compounded by the fear of many others that they would get "it" too. Overnight, apathy became hysteria.*[132]

Though the panic never fully subsided, the general public has, largely as a result of the CDC's efforts, become aware of at least basic steps toward prevention. Though the CDC took a lot of heat for linking AIDS with a homosexual lifestyle, it was also key in identifying the other forms of contraction and, in turn, providing the public with preventive measures. Through the years, medicine has greatly advanced, and AIDS is no longer the assured death sentence it once was. Especially after it became clear that the disease was, in fact, not just a homosexual disease, the CDC has continued to stress the importance of avoiding intravenous drug use and promiscuous sex as paramount for prevention, and the importance of testing in order to limit new cases.

Never before had the world turned its attention to Druid Hills as it did after September 11, 2001. Immediately, the threat of bioterrorism skyrocketed and the CDC found itself at the center of national defense. Since 1999, the CDC had been in charge of preparing cities and states for a potential bioterrorist attack. Before 9/11, the job, though an important one, had been on a drastically smaller scale, as the typical grant allocated to a city or state was about $500,000 annually. Post–9/11, that number rose to an average of $13 million. National disaster had also brought awareness of the need for increased security and renovations to the headquarters on Clifton Road, which looked like pretty easy pickings for a terrorist attack. Besides leading prevention efforts, the CDC was charged with investigating the increasing number of cases of anthrax poisoning, which had made the most routine acts, such as opening mail, one more thing to fear. Though much attention was paid to its failure to solve the mystery of where the anthrax was coming from, the CDC's adeptness in recognizing those who were at risk for anthrax poisoning, and quickly treating them, likely saved hundreds of lives.[133]

On a visit to the CDC less than a month after 9/11, President Bush echoed this opinion. "I truly believe you saved hundreds of lives, and for that I am grateful," he said to the anthrax task force, calling them the "new heroes of America."[134] President Bush has since proposed multiple cutbacks for federal funding of the CDC. As of May 2007, the CDC's annual budget was about $9.2 billion. While Director Julie Gerberding proposed a $1 billion increase in funds for the 2008 year, President Bush favored cutting the budget by half that amount.[135] While the CDC's future remains as uncertain as other questions with which it is faced (Will we have a cure for AIDS in twenty-five years? Is reimplementing the smallpox vaccine as a safeguard against possible bioterrorism worth the risks?), one thing is certain, at least in regard to Druid Hills: no matter what direction it takes, the CDC's headquarters is by far the most globally significant landmark, not only within the neighborhood, but within Atlanta as a whole.

VA hospital

In December 2007, Congress passed a measure allowing for up to $21 million for renovations on the Veterans Administration Hospital located at 1670 Clairmont Road.[136] Its location only makes sense, as Clairmont Road is also named Pete Wheeler Highway after the commissioner of the Georgia Department of Veteran Services. Wheeler still works a full day, despite having served as commissioner since 1949. That same year, Wheeler and his lovely wife Gerry built their home in Druid Hills. One of Druid Hills' unsung heroes, the former army infantryman was also elected chairman of the World War II Memorial Advisory Board by the president, and he served in that capacity until the memorial was completed in 2004.[137]

At the turn of the century, after thirty-three years in midtown Atlanta, the VA's regional office moved to the same site as the hospital in Druid Hills. The office handles benefit claims, pensions, home loan guarantees and educational and vocational rehabilitation services.[138] It is located next to the hospital, which has 173 beds in its medical unit, and an additional 100 beds in the nursing home unit. It also houses an extensive research program with over three hundred projects as of 2007. One of six hospitals associated with Emory University, the VA provides care for Georgians who have sacrificed much for this country. Especially at a time when some VA hospitals have come under attack for their substandard conditions, this one is an institution that Druid Hills' residents should take great pride in.

Chapter 7

DHCA

Preserving Olmsted's Principles

The spectrum of opinion on the Druid Hills Civic Association (DHCA) is broad. On one hand, the group is seen as a neighborhood watchman that rules with an iron fist—prospective developers whose attempts to break ground in the neighborhood have been thwarted, and residents seeking to make additions to their property are examples of those who often share this opinion. Then there are the DHCA members, as well as their admirers, who see the group as paramount to preserving the historical neighborhood and the only line of defense capable of standing up to developers who would turn the spacious, green lots into their own Levittown (post–World War II Long Island, New York town with approximately seventeen thousand homes on only a thousand acres of land). William Levitt described his approach to developing as channeling "labor and materials to a stationary outdoor assembly line instead of bringing them together inside a factory"[139] if it turns a profit.

Regardless of where one falls on this spectrum, one must be impressed with the vigor and dedication that fuels the association, as well as with the results they have achieved. The DHCA website (www.druidhills.org) gives, in effect, a mission statement:

> *The Druid Hills Civic Association was founded in 1938 to preserve the Druid Hills neighborhood for high quality residential use and to protect the unique heritage of the area. The Association carries out these responsibilities by exercising vigilance in zoning matters, maintaining a liaison with local governing bodies, informing the citizens of community problems, and promoting the general welfare of the community for the enjoyment of its residents today and in the future.*

While the wording of the aforementioned is not unusual for a civic group, what sets the DHCA apart is its ability to put the above into effect.

Former DHCA president Mike Terry notes that "most (neighborhood organizations) are quite incapable of litigating against a large corporation…You can organize neighborhood opposition, you can lobby your commission, but when it comes time to go to court and do battle…you can't do it." One Emory faculty member was also impressed, stating, "They are extremely savvy and well connected, and they know the process and they know how to effect change. You certainly have to work with them, or they may work against you. I have to respect the efforts they undertake to preserve their neighborhood, because it's a beautiful neighborhood."[140]

Some critics of the DHCA consider it an elitist group aimed at isolating Druid Hills from necessary changes brought on by the growth of Atlanta. Accordingly, it was the DHCA that incurred much of the blame for MARTA's (Metropolitan Atlanta Rapid Transit Authority) abandonment of light rail proposals for DeKalb County. The association opposed a proposal that would have created a route, using the existing CSX railroad line, which runs parallel to Haygood Drive at the intersection of Clifton Road, to connect Emory with the Lindbergh MARTA station and Northlake Mall.[141]

Another issue, that of the Jerusalem House, placed the DHCA in a most precarious position. In a move that could not be less politically correct, it staunchly opposed the purchase of the house at 831 Briarcliff Road by the directors of the Jerusalem House, a home for up to twenty-four AIDS patients who otherwise would be homeless. Opposition originally centered around two concerns: first, the DHCA took issue with the definition of the Jerusalem House concerning the permitted uses of multi-family zoning that applies to Briarcliff. At the time, Briarcliff on the Druid Hills side was an Urban Conservation District. A special committee of the DHCA came up with an endorsement of a much smaller facility—a residence using the existing house for people with AIDS. Also present was the concern that intravenous drug use, a common way of contracting HIV, might pose a threat to the well-being of the neighborhood. Evelyn Ullman, board president for the Jerusalem House, pledged that no medical treatment would take place, and therefore the home could not be considered an "institution." Furthermore, Ullman stressed that keeping a drug-free home was of the highest concern, and measures would be taken to that effect.[142]

In 1989, the Atlanta City Council Zoning Committee voted in favor of the Jerusalem House, and plans for renovation got underway. In November 1989, the Jerusalem House welcomed its first tenants: four male AIDS sufferers with no home and nowhere else to go. It is, of course, important to keep in mind the drastic change in the way the disease is looked upon today as compared to how it was perceived in 1989. At that time, treatment was less effective and carriers were often shunned in the same way as lepers once were. Therefore, it was easy for people outside of Druid Hills to shake their heads from afar, yet one would be hard-pressed to find any neighborhood at the time that would embrace a home for AIDS patients with open arms.

The civic association also opposed a second branch of the Jerusalem House for single mothers with AIDS and their children. The proposed home was the former Davidson School across from the North Decatur Road entrance to Lullwater Drive. Despite its original opposition, the DHCA reached a compromise with the Jerusalem House, an agreement which allowed for occupancy provided there was no expansion to the existing building and no medical practice on the property. Again, it is easy for today's removed spectator to look at the DHCA with disgust for its opposition to such a humane cause, but at the time the project was proposed, AIDS was a death sentence plain and simple. Had the Jerusalem House tried to locate in any other neighborhood, one can be certain that opposition would have been raised from that neighborhood's residents. Furthermore, the DHCA never objected to the home on the basis that its tenants had AIDS; they objected to the precedent that such an establishment could create, making intrusion from institutions more likely.

The DHCA has not always been able to stop undesirable development. I am referring to the 4.1 acres of land once occupied by one of Druid Hills' finest homes, then called "Paradiso." Built in 1923, and undoubtedly inspired by a recent trip to Italy with his mentor Neel Reid, Lewis Edmund "Buck" Crook Jr. built this Italian Renaissance villa, which stood overlooking the Olmsted parks, at 1695 South Ponce de Leon Avenue. This picturesque abode characterized the diversity of Crook's designs—compare it with the Tudor style employed in W.T. Candler's Lullwater House—as well as the concern he had for maintaining design principles, such as "right proportions of masses and scale of details."[143]

Neighbors and passersby watched the gorgeous villa degenerate into a "haven for vagrants and a reputed den of devil worship" by the 1960s. In 1976, the city of Atlanta demolished the home after a woman was gang raped there.[144] Tom Harrison knew he had a difficult task ahead of him when he entered contract negotiations to purchase the land. For years prior, developers had tried and failed to build on the property, which had been protected as part of Druid Hills Historic District since 1982. As a result, Harrison would need approval from the Atlanta Urban Design Commission (UDC) and the Board of Zoning Adjustment for proposed reductions on side yard setbacks: thirty to twenty feet on the interior, and fifty to thirty feet on the Clifton Road side. The proposed twenty-one homes were seen as "several orders of magnitude better than the previous plans we have seen for the site," said one UDC member. But, as another remarked, the design of the homes was "inappropriate for the area." The UDC's original recommendation was that Harrison reroute several roads within the project and place four of the homes together in the front of the development, in order to provide the façade of a single-family home to passersby on Ponce de Leon.[145]

Originally, DHCA members worked alongside Harrison in order to ensure that plans were created in accord with Olmsted's principles. This relationship soured after the UDC approved plans for what they claimed to have thought were two-story units, but when built were three-story units. Harrison claimed that it was an innocent mistake, but when "innocent mistakes" include building units in a historic district that are a third higher than the developer had in his own plans, questions of sincerity, as well as competence, naturally arise. The UDC continued to approve zoning variances in July 1989. At the time, only seven of the eighteen (part of a revised proposal, which reduced the number of units from twenty-one to eighteen) proposed homes were completed, yet Harrison was already asking for and receiving permission for variances allowing development to encroach upon neighboring property.[146]

This trend continued, and by the time development was complete, Dr. Marion Kuntz had a ten-foot-high wall encroaching on her property line, in blatant violation of the rule

Courtesy of the Special Collections Department and Archives, Georgia State University Library.

This Italian villa, built for Mr. and Mrs. F.O. Stone, can be attributed to the time Crook spent with Reid in Italy during their 1922 European Tour. *Courtesy of the Special Collections Department and Archives, Georgia State University Library.*

stating that thirty feet must be left between any new building and a historic property. I had the privilege of spending an afternoon with the regents professor and prolific author at her home adjacent to the Paradiso. The beautiful brick home was designed by acclaimed architect Philip Trammell Shutze of the "Georgia School of Classicists"[147] and a disciple of Reid. Originally built for Dr. John Hurt, brother of Joel, the house is a treasure, featuring Flemish bond—the style of alternating horizontal bricks with vertical bricks, creating thicker walls and an exceptional color contrast between the standard red brick facing one way, and a dark blue, almost grey, brick facing the other.

It was interesting to see for myself how the Paradiso buildings towered over Dr. Kuntz's property, as well as the areas of her house that had suffered damage from flooding, silt deposits and accumulation of mud—all of this in blatant violation of historic zoning laws according to which it is illegal to raise the land. Dr. Kuntz described the effects of Paradiso on her property as "drastic, all in a negative sense." She continued,

Now, the only place I can see around the towers they built is in my dining room. I was never opposed to development, as long as it happened within the law. I called the city of Atlanta every day to tell them the developers were breaking zoning laws, and nothing happened. Now I can't have privacy on my own back terrace if I want to read out there during the summer.[148]

For the purpose of this work—a separate work would be required to detail all of the DHCA's battles—we will focus on the most significant DHCA battle as it relates to Atlanta as a whole. Beginning in July of 1981, with former President Jimmy Carter's announcement that he intended to locate his presidential library in the soon to be developed Great Park, the DHCA entered into a decade-long battle, which pitted it against Mayor Andrew Young, the department of transportation and the "man from Plains." This was a daunting task, especially since, as Atlanta historian Dana F. White points out, "Carter did not show himself to be the saintly figure he is seen as today. He played real hardball."[149]

White says this in regard to the proposed Presidential Parkway, a 2.4-mile road that would connect Ponce de Leon with the downtown connector. According to the proposed plans, the road would cut through Candler, Goldsboro, Shady Side and Dellwood Parks, and required that 7.8 acres of park space be condemned.[150]

While campaigning for the 1981 mayoral election, former ambassador to the United Nations (under Carter) Andrew Young took a stand against new, multilane roads in Atlanta. However, upon his election, his tone quickly changed, as evident by his proposal for the new parkway. In 1982 CAUTION (Citizens Against Unnecessary Thoroughfares in Older Neighborhoods) was formed to unite neighborhood groups against the proposed parkway. The DHCA was, of course, an important member of CAUTION. That September, the Atlanta Regional Commission voted thirteen to seven in favor of adding the proposed parkway into the overall metro transportation plan. In late 1984, U.S. District Judge William O'Kelley ruled against an attempt by CAUTION to stop the parkway. Construction was beginning to seem inevitable. As a result, in

February 1985 a group of protestors, calling themselves "Roadbusters," formed a "tent city" in Shady Side Park, camping out and chaining themselves to trees where the proposed road would run.[151]

O'Kelley's ruling stated that the Federal Highway Administration's (FHA) environmental impact study of the proposed parkway met federal environmental guidelines. CAUTION then appealed O'Kelley's decision to the Eleventh U.S. Circuit Court of Appeals, which gave parkway opponents some hope when it ruled that the government must further study the road's impact. The FHA complied with the ruling, and in late 1986, it sent the revised study to O'Kelley, who again ruled in favor of the study. Inevitably, an appeal was filed on the grounds that the study on environmental impact was inadequate, and alternatives to the parkway were not mentioned. December 1987 saw the Georgia Department of Transportation score a major victory when the eleventh circuit ruled on the appeal, this time upholding O'Kelley's ruling.[152]

In 1986, the State Commission on the Condemnation of Property was formed in response to DeKalb County Superior Court Judge Clarence Seeliger's ruling that the DOT did not have the authority to condemn land owned by another government. This turned out to be a crucial decision in the parkway battle. Another petition to condemn land was not filed until July of 1988. The tide was beginning to turn in favor of the DHCA and its fellow neighborhood organizations. The Carter Center, which broke ground in 1984, was falling short on traffic projections. This tended to support opponents' arguments that the road was an unnecessary allocation of government funds. Lagging traffic projections were compounded with allegations that former commissioner Tom Moreland had ordered members of his staff to adjust the projections to levels on par with the original expectations.[153]

The year 1988 was proving to be a good one for CAUTION. DeKalb County commissioner Sherry Sutton proposed a resolution calling for DeKalb County's "vigorous opposition" to the parkway. The county commission voted in favor of the measure, four to three. But victory was short-lived, as DeKalb's chief executive officer Manuel Maloof vetoed the resolution, stating that DeKalb County "has never taken a position in diametric opposition to a city within our boundaries, as this resolution does with respect to the city of Atlanta. To do so now would create a dangerous precedent and one which may well work to the detriment of the county in the future."[154]

That same year, Judge Seeliger ordered a stop to all parkway construction within DeKalb County, until the issue of land condemnation was resolved. Parkway supporters were getting antsy, realizing that, regardless of the victor in the upcoming mayoral election—be it Michael Lomax or Maynard Jackson—he would oppose the parkway.

Seeliger was a constant thorn in parkway supporters' sides. Feeling the sting of bias, the state issued a petition that recommended his removal from the parkway case. The petition resulted in a bit of a Catch-22 when Seeliger himself rejected the petition, admitting to no sort of prejudice. DeKalb Superior Court Judge John W. Hilford was charged with overseeing an appeal from the state's attorney general's office that argued that Seeliger was unable to make a fair decision on an issue pertaining to himself. Hilford reviewed the evidence and ruled in favor of the judge.

Despite years of litigation in the courts, neither CAUTION and its counterparts nor the DOT saw the possibility of fruitful negotiations. If he could negotiate peace between Egypt and Israel, surely Carter could negotiate such a minor dispute as this. In late 1989, Carter met with, among others, DOT commissioner Hal Rives, who admitted afterwards that the state might be willing to meet with the neighborhood groups. The former president also attempted mediation with Judge Seeliger, whom he admonished in the press: "He is supposed to be an objective judge, but I don't think there is any question he is highly biased against the parkway." Carter convinced Seeliger to ask parkway opponents how they felt about Seeliger's personally meeting with Carter. According to Carter, Seeliger told him that they declined. CAUTION stated its position on the matter, declaring that talks between the two men were perfectly fine as long as they went on in open court and not in private.[155] Despite failure to negotiate, the pendulum was starting to swing in Carter's favor. In December 1990 the state supreme court reversed Judge Seeliger's ruling that the state did not have authority to condemn land. No doubt the ruling was a major victory for the parkway, but a few issues still remained unresolved. First, there was the litigation pending between the DOT and Cox Broadcasting concerning which of the two was responsible for ice falling from television antenna cables that ran above the proposed road. The Cox company owned the cables, but they posed no threat unless the road was created. The matters of whether the DOT used inflated traffic counts, and what the value was of the condemned land, were also pending. The resolution was all the more superfluous insofar as it would be Seeliger presiding over these two disputes.

Whether the DOT reported false traffic counts in the past, in 1990, attendance numbers for the Carter Center decreased substantially for the third straight year since its opening in 1987. In its inaugural year, the Carter Center hosted over 190,000 visitors. By 1990, the number dwindled to just under 80,000.[156] The decline further exasperated the parkway's supporters and was partially responsible for the DOT's decision that negotiation was inevitable. Another likely reason for negotiation was the upcoming Olympics. The last thing state officials needed, coming on the heels of the announcement that Atlanta would host the 1996 Olympics, was an unfinished parkway when visitors flooded the city. Completion of the parkway before the start of the Olympics was crucial, especially if the Carter Center was to attract tourists. Essentially, the DHCA and the rest of CAUTION had postponed development long enough that, with no end in sight, the state agreed to open talks with the neighborhood groups in February 1991.

Talks between the two sides began in February 1991 and were successfully mediated by the Neighborhood Justice Center of Atlanta Inc.—a nonprofit group that specialized in conflict resolution. A total of nine meetings took place, the last of which came in late August the same year. With the agreement on a plan developed by Leon Eplan, Atlanta's commissioner of planning and development, the DHCA succeeded in assuring that its beloved Olmsted parks would not be touched. The plan allowed for a four-lane surface street connecting the downtown connector with the Carter Center, followed by two lanes that circle the center and then meet on the east side and run to Moreland Avenue. This was CAUTION's biggest victory in the dispute as the road was originally to run past Moreland, through the parks to Ponce de Leon, gobbling up almost eight acres of parkland in the process.[157]

Olmsted's influence on Druid Hills was safe. The importance of park space in Olmsted's design was briefly mentioned earlier, but it now requires further attention. Olmsted separated the public recreation that parks sought to provide into two categories: *exertive* and *receptive*. The first is composed of "games chiefly of mental skill, as chess, or athletic sports, as baseball." The second, and more important of the two, is composed of "all which cause us to receive pleasure without conscious exertion."

Receptive recreation has two further subdivisions: *gregarious* and *neighborly*. *Gregarious* recreation occurs when large groups meet in a public setting, in order to enjoy one another's company. Olmstedian thought maintains that "it does men good to come together in this way in pure air and under the light of heaven" in order to counteract the "ordinary hard, hustling working hours of town life." Olmsted observed true *gregarious* recreation and described it as "not at all intellectual, competitive with none, disposing to jealousy and spiritual or intellectual pride toward none, each individual adding by his mere presence to the pleasure of all others, all helping to the greater happiness of each." *Neighborly* recreation occurs in smaller, intimate groups and "without stimulating exertion; and the close relation of family life, the association of children, of mothers, of lovers, or those who may be lovers, stimulate and keep alive the more tender sympathies, and give play to faculties such as may be dormant in business or on the promenade."

Park space is vital for these forms of recreation, without which individuals cannot take leave of the evils and ugliness often present in city life. Parks should be designed on

> *ground to which people may easily go after their day's work is done, and where they may stroll for an hour…where they shall, in effect, find the city put far away from them. We want, especially, the greatest possible contrast with the restraining and confining conditions of the town, those conditions which compel us to walk circumspectly, watchfully, jealously, which compel us to look closely upon others without sympathy.*[158]

The Presidential Parkway threat had revitalized interest in Atlanta's parks. The DHCA had spent the past decade fighting for the six parks, which bore the imprint of the "father of landscape architecture" in a city with virtually no park space compared to other major cities within the United States. Once the parks were saved from the bulldozers, Druid Hills residents were able to take a collective breath and enjoy what they had fought for so vigilantly. What they quickly realized was that the linear park that had drawn so much attention in the courts and in the media was in dire need of attention to its grounds. Parkway issues had necessitated such time, money and effort that maintaining upkeep, as well as adhering to Olmstedian principles, was lost in the struggle. Trees were dying, carefully laid out shrubbery was marred with mimosa and privet, eyesores including large playground equipment and an athletic field added to drainage problems resulting in large patches of dead grass—all of this would have caused Olmsted to cringe.

The DHCA took action, along with the Olmsted Parks Society of Atlanta (OLPA), Park Pride and the Druid Hills Garden Club, by developing the Olmsted Linear Park Master Plan in 1995. (The parks, along with the Ponce de Leon Parkway, were listed on the National

Register of Historic Places in 1975.) The original master plan for restoration was developed by the Atlanta firm Altamira and the noted New York landscape architecture firm of Quennell Rothschild, especially Nicholas Quennell. Charles Beveridge, likely the foremost authority on Olmsted, was one of many consultants employed to ensure that the new plan adhered to Olmsted's original plan. Plans were adopted in 1997 by the city of Atlanta, DeKalb County and Fernbank, the three bodies sharing maintenance responsibilities for the parks. Atlanta maintains Springdale, Oak Grove, Shady Side and Virgilee Parks, while Deepdene and Dellwood are owned by Fernbank, yet treated as public parks and maintained by DeKalb County.

Shortly thereafter, the landscape architectural firm Tunnell and Tunnell Inc. began a makeover of Oak Grove Park. Steps in restoring the park were carefully taken, in keeping with the original plan. They included burying power lines, planting new grass, repairing and adding new curbs and installing light fixtures. Harking back to the original design, trees were restored around the edge of the park, which serve as buffers from the sights and sounds of the city as well as providing shade and tranquility. Many shrubs were planted, following the Olmsted firm's planting plan of 1905, with careful adjustment for current botanical and social considerations. The work of Tunnell and Tunnell also involved replanning and constructing the interior pathway that the Olmsted firm had designed. Renovation on Oak Grove was completed in May 2001, and work began on Dellwood, Shady Side and Virgilee.

Fundraising was integral to the park's restoration. OLPA fundraising projects, including galas and garage sales, raised privately donated funds, while millions in public funds were raised, ironically, due in no small part to the efforts of the DOT. State Transportation Commissioner Harold Linnenkohl, speaking at the November 2003 dedication of the second phase of the parks, announced that "the department of transportation isn't just about building roads. This is probably the most important program we have statewide—park settings and restoring waterfront areas on the coast."[159] Fifteen years earlier, the idea of the DOT commissioner speaking at an Olmsted Park dedication seemed about as likely as General Sherman speaking at the ribbon-cutting for the state capitol. Nothing says "I'm sorry" like money, however, and with a recent survey by the Trust for Public Land and the Urban Land Institute announcing that Atlanta sets aside less land for park space than any major city in the country, the DOT decided it fit to become a friend to the parks.[160]

When the second phase was completed, the three parks, Dellwood, Shady Side and Virgilee, had undergone improvements similar to those made on Oak Grove. The two phases saw the creation of six thousand linear feet of pathways and the planting of twenty-six hundred new plants and trees. Signs were also placed around the parks to identify different park segments and provide historical background. A total of $4.2 million was spent on the first two phases, the most costly of which was the burial of some eleven miles of utility line.[161]

Springdale Park also benefited from the second phase. Utility lines were buried, curbs were repaired and lighting was added. Trees, new grass and shrubbery were subsequently planted in the 5.2-acre park. Further renovation included the removal of a playground—built in the 1930s, it was an intrusion on the park's natural, expansive area—and the development of a play area that was unobtrusive to the park's natural scenery.

Ongoing is the last phase of the project, the renovation of Deepdene Park—the largest of the six, comprising twenty-two acres, much of which is forest. Approximately $4 million is the expected cost for improvements, which are slated for completion sometime around late 2008. Aside from burying utility lines, building curbs, et cetera, Tunnell and Tunnell is charged with creating walking trails, allowing for public access to the heavily wooded area, as well as restoring Peavine Creek, which bisects the property. Work will also be done removing intrusive shrubs prevalent in wooded areas suffering from neglect.[162]

Perhaps if government bodies such as the DOT had cared as much about Peavine Creek in the early 1990s as they do now, another preservation effort by Druid Hills residents would have ended differently. In 1992, Sam Jones sold thirty-six acres of forest resting between Fernbank Elementary School and Druid Hills High School to developers Parks Chewning and Warner Blair for $4.2 million. Jones had inherited Durand Farm from his late wife, the final heir to the property. One of the few forests remaining in the city, it had been in her family for six generations and provided a sanctuary where the sound of chirping birds and running streams offered a temporary reprieve from the sounds of concrete slowly creeping in.

In October of 1992, Peavine Creek flood risks were among the reasons DHCA members cited in a suit against the developers, claiming that their preliminary plat failed in sufficiently addressing adverse effects on the neighborhood. The ensuing rule set a precedent that a county law, which according to the judge had been ignored since 1956, stated that preliminary plans for development must be approved by a planning committee, not the planning director, as was the case in the Durand Farm issue. As a result, the DeKalb County Planning Commission was ordered to rule on a preliminary plat for the first time. Members of the eight-person board were less than thrilled with the added burden, as commissioner Bob Lundsten protested, "I don't know who would take the job of planning commissioner [in DeKalb] if this procedure is changed to where we have to approve all plats."[163]

Bill Crecelius Jr., attorney for Chewning and Blair, had countersued the DHCA for $10 million in December 1992 (eventually dropped), and now was threatening to file suit against the Planning Commission, citing that each day the project was delayed cost his clients thousands of dollars, and that the DHCA opposition had damaged public opinion surrounding the project.[164]

According to staff writer Shelley Emling, who covered the proceedings for the *Atlanta Journal-Constitution*, the Planning Commission acted "under the threat of a lawsuit" when voting unanimously to approve a preliminary plan for development of seventy-one houses rather than the eighty-two that had been proposed. Emling noted that the commission had, earlier in the February 3 meeting, voted four to three to deny the plan, but had "changed their vote without explanation after a 40 minute executive session."[165]

The commission denied eleven of the lots because they were on a flood plain. Yet, in a final victory for developers, Superior Court Judge Daniel M. Coursey ruled that all eighty-two houses could be built after Blair and Chewning cited a law allowing for building if a minimum of 70 percent of said property lies outside the flood plain.[166] By December 1993, houses were already springing up on the once pure land.

So, were Druid Hills residents merely stalling when they filed suit against the developers, or would the Durand Mill subdivision have adverse affects on the environment? In an editorial written four years after Durand Mill materialized, Katie Baer described the adverse effects in her own backyard. A "mature red oak" fell across a strip of Peavine Creek running through her backyard. She notes that it was "obvious that clear-cutting of dozens of acres of the old Durand Mill property to build an enclave of half-million-dollar houses and destruction of wetlands would have a cost." Compounding this was the fact that a swimming pool, tennis courts and paved parking were added to the property in lieu of a retention pond. Consequently, Peavine Creek was affected by further runoff, causing rapidly increased erosion on its banks that, in turn, weakened the soil's hold on the old trees.[167]

The DHCA succeeded in saving, revitalizing and maintaining the Olmsted Linear Park. Yet, unfortunately Durand Farm was one piece of beautiful, wooded land that could not be saved from the developer.

I used to work on a landscaping job with several clients in Druid Hills. I remember one sweltering summer day we had just finished work on a home off Lullwater and were heading toward the last house of the day on Princeton Way. Sweat had already claimed my original T-shirt (the second T-shirt of the day always reminded me I was close to delirium) when my coworker Elliot turned onto Princeton. Looking up, squinting through the imposing sun's rays, I saw something that made me sure that I had heatstroke: a turkey about five feet from being run over! Then another one and another one! One can't imagine my relief when Elliot, who was driving, uttered a two-word expletive, assuring me I was not hallucinating. There were actually three turkeys trotting about as if they owned the place.

What I learned that day was one of Druid Hills' little enigmas—that these *Meleagris gallopavos* (a.k.a. wild turkeys) have been accepted guests in the neighborhood for decades. One of the theories as to where they came from suggests that they once inhabited the Durand property, but were forced out by development.[168]

A wildlife biologist who studied the turkeys concluded that Druid Hills' natural environment has everything on a turkey's menu—bugs, plant buds, the occasional lizard and berries.[169] It does not appear that the turkeys are going anywhere any time soon, so just drive carefully on Emory Drive, Princeton Way and Durand Drive, as our feathered guests do not seem to be afraid of cars.

Notes

Introduction

1. Peter Applebome, "Atlanta: Scenes Beyond the Mall," *New York Times*, June 2, 1996.
2. Karen Hill, "Cleanup Effort at Historic Cemetery Showing Results," *Atlanta Journal Constitution*, June 26, 2003, JA/4.
3. Ibid.
4. Kurtz, "Map of the Battle."

Chapter 1: Designing According to Nature

5. "Joel Hurt's Role Astonishes his Friends," *Atlanta Constitution*, June 3, 1905, 5.
6. Lyon, "Frederick Law Olmsted," 180–83.
7. Edge, *Joel Hurt*.
8. U.S. Census Bureau, www.census.gov.
9. Frederick Law Olmsted to John C. Olmsted, March 13, 1894, Olmsted Papers.
10. Lyon, "Frederick Law Olmsted," 165–190.
11. Hall, *Olmsted's America*.
12. Roth, "Frederick Law Olmsted's First and Last Suburbs."
13. Ibid.
14. Fisher, *Frederick Law Olmsted*.
15. Frederick Law Olmsted and Company to Joel Hurt, December 5, 1890, Olmsted Papers.
16. Fisher, *Frederick Law Olmsted*.

Chapter 2: The Druid Hills Company

17. "Q&A," *Atlanta Journal-Constitution*, May 15, 2006, B/2

18. Bowditch, *Druid Hill Park*.

19. "Syndicate Buys Big Land Tract," *Atlanta Constitution*, 1908, 6.

20. "Buyers Tell of Money Lost on Adair Bonds," *Atlanta Constitution*, November 28, 1928, 1.

21. "Adairs Petition to Incorporate," *Atlanta Constitution*, March 21, 1920.

22. Candler, *Asa Griggs Candler*.

23. "Forrest Adair Busy in Candler Campaign," *Atlanta Constitution*, August 12, 1916, 5.

24. "100,000 Worth of Lots Sold at Druid Hills," *Atlanta Constitution*, February 21, 1909, B/7.

25. "Many Handsome Homes to go up in Druid Hills," *Atlanta Constitution*, September 22, 1908.

26. Lyon, "Frederick Law Olmsted," 165–190.

27. "Forrest Adair Buys Big Tract of Land," *Atlanta Constitution*, February 16, 1910, 3.

28. Lyon, "Frederick Law Olmsted," 165–190.

29. "Handsome Home to be Erected by Massengale," *Atlanta Constitution*, November 2, 1919.

30. "Robinson Purchases Forrest Adair's Home," *Atlanta Constitution*, August 29, 1919.

31. "Adairs Petition to Incorporate."

32. "Building Outlook Continues Bright, Declares Adair," *Atlanta Constitution*, August 26, 1923, E/8.

33. Ibid.

34. "Druid Hills Sales Setting Records," *Atlanta Constitution*, January 23, 1927, B/4.

35. "Building Outlook Continues Bright, Declares Adair," *Atlanta Constitution*, August 26, 1923, E/8.

36. "74,000 People Pack 'Homes Beautiful' as Exhibit Closes," *Atlanta Constitution*, April 5, 1926, 1.

37. "Dekalb to Give Police Protection to Druid Hills," *Atlanta Constitution*, April 1, 1928, 10/A.

38. "Druid Hills Bus Line Authorized," *Atlanta Constitution*, October 24, 1929, 1.

39. Mitchell, *Lewis Edmund Crook, Jr.*

40. "Druid Hills Drives for Fire Protection," *Atlanta Constitution*, April 4, 1933, 10.

41. "Tax, Fire Rate Cuts Sought in Druid Hills Incorporation," *Atlanta Constitution*, February 5, 1933, 2/A.

42. "Druid Hills Bill Lost as Governor Vetoes Measure," *Atlanta Constitution*, March 25, 1933, 1.

43. "Druid Hills Fire Tax Approved by House," *Atlanta Constitution*, March 19, 1937, 1.

44. "Stars to Attend Opening of Lullwater Race Course," *Atlanta Constitution*, April 26, 1922, 13.

45. George Congdon, "Lullwater Farm Christened at Presidents' Club Outing," *Atlanta Constitution*, June 8, 1924, B/1.

46. Mi-Harness.net, "Harness Racing and Standardbreds in North America and Michigan," www.mi-harness.com.

47. "Animals Arrive Today for Asa Candler Zoo," *Atlanta Constitution*, April 20, 1932, 1.

48. "Asa Candler Buys Score of Animals for Private Zoo," *Atlanta Constitution*, March 2, 1932, 4.

49. "Druid Hills Residents ask Asa G. Candler to Remove Zoo," *Atlanta Constitution*, August 6, 1932, 1.

50. Ibid.

51. "Candler, in First Statement on Zoo, Denies Neighbors' Nuisance Charges," *Atlanta Constitution*, August 12, 1932, 1.

52. "Asa Candler Zoo Sued for $25,000," *Atlanta Constitution*, March 2, 1933, 6.

53. "Man is Arrested in Extortion Plot Against Candler," *Atlanta Constitution*, March 1, 1933, 1.

54. Robert Bunnelle, "Front Yard Zoo of Asa Candler is Running Husky Winter Deficit," *Atlanta Constitution*, December 23, 1934, 2/C.

55. "Right to Levy $100 Per Day Tax on Candler Zoo Upheld in Ruling," *Atlanta Constitution*, February 25, 1934, 6/C.

56. "Candler Dismisses Curator of Zoo, Seeks to Sell Animal Collection," *Atlanta Constitution*, September 21, 1933, 1.

Chapter 3: Architecture

57. Mitchell, *Lewis Edmund Crook, Jr.*

58. Ibid.

59. Ibid.

60. Bryson, *History of Lullwater.*

61. Mitchell, *J. Neel Reid.*

62. Ibid.

63. "Neel Reid Passes At Roswell Home," *Atlanta Constitution*, February 15, 1926: 1.

64. "Young Architect Joins Local Firm," *Atlanta Constitution*, May 2, 1926: 6.

65. Dowling, *American Classicist.*

66. William Mitchell, interview by Robert Hartle, September 2007.

67. "Young Atlanta Architect Wins Rome Scholarship in Nation-Wide Contest," *Atlanta Constitution*, June 27, 1915, C/9.

68. Dowling, *American Classicist.*

69. New Georgia Encyclopedia, s.v. "Smith, Francis Palmer," http://www.georgiaencyclopedia. org/nge/Article.jsp?id=h-569 (accessed October 5, 2007).

70. Susan Summers, interview by Robert Hartle, September 15, 2007.

Chapter 4: Good Substantial People in Moderate Circumstances

71. "Homes Sell Fast in Emory Grove," *Atlanta Constitution*, December 17, 1939, 11/K.
72. Molly Thomson, "Spotlight On...Emory Grove," *Atlanta Journal-Constitution*, June 25, 2006, HF/8.
73. Pete and Gerry Wheeler, interview by Robert Hartle, June 28, 2007.
74. White, "Foreword."
75. Howard Pousner, "Classic Theatre has Seen Several Remakes," *Atlanta Journal-Constitution*, September 1, 2006, H/6.
76. Gournay, *AIA Guide*.
77. Ben Smith III, "Druid Hills Civic Association: Long on History, Clout," *Atlanta Journal-Constitution*, May 1, 2000, B/1.
78. "Negro Highwaymen Hold up Street Car and Shoot Crew," *Atlanta Journal*, April 24, 1910, B/1.
79. "Negroes Saved by Technicality," *Atlanta Constitution*, November 16, 1910, 1.
80. Ibid.
81. "One Druid Hills Murderer set Free," *Atlanta Constitution*, March 16, 1911, 9.
82. Jordan, *Murder in the Peach State*.
83. Ibid.
84. Ibid.

Chapter 5: Creating Cultural Community

85. James A. Mackay, "Glenn Memorial United Methodist Church," http://www.glennumc.org/history.htm.
86. Carribel R. Blankinship, "Tremendous Growth in Druid Hills Baptist Sunday School, Atlanta, Georgia," *Sunday School Builder* (July 1930), 13–14.
87. Martha Manning, interview by Robert Hartle, May 15, 2007.
88. "Sam H. Venable's Druid Hills Home Fulfills Dream of Twenty-Five Years," *Atlanta Constitution*, October 19, 1913, 4.
89. "Pinebloom is Now Church," *Atlanta Journal*, May 13, 1973.
90. Sarah Cash, "Let There Be Lights, Camera, Action: Druid Hills Church Becomes Temporary Motion Picture Set," *Atlanta Journal-Constitution*, April 28, 1988, A/1.
91. Gayle White, "Quaker House Losing Friends: Group has Outgrown Place of Worship," *Atlanta Journal-Constitution*, May 1, 1989, B/1.
92. Gayle White, *Atlanta Journal-Constitution*, September 6, 1996, C/3.
93. Mary M. Byrne, *Atlanta Journal-Constitution*, June 5, 2004, B/1.
94. "Druid Hills Club Formally Opened Wednesday Morning," *Atlanta Constitution*, April 30, 1914, 5.
95. Druid Hills Golf Club, "History of Druid Hills," http://www.dhgc.org/club/scripts/library/view_document.asp?grp=9087&ns=public&app=80&dn=history.

96. Paul Warwick, "Barbeque at Druid Hills Enjoyed by Opera Stars," *Atlanta Constitution*, April 29, 1920, 11.

97. Fernbank Museum of Natural History, "History," http://www.fernbankmuseum.org/museum_info/about/history.aspx.

98. Eric Sundquist and Jill Young Miller, "Fernbank Museum of Natural History Still Struggles After Battling Its Way Back From the Brink," *Atlanta Journal-Constitution*, May 29, 2001, A/1.

99. Elizabeth Lenhard, "Fernbank Opens $43 Million Museum," *Atlanta Journal-Constitution*, October 6, 1992, C/3.

100. Sundquist and Miller, "Fernbank Museum," *Atlanta Journal-Constitution*, A/1.

101. "Audience at School Hears W.D. Thompson Speech," *Dekalb New Era*, September 27, 1951.

102. Richard Sams, "A History of Druid Hills High School," presentation to the Reunion of the Class of 1956. Available online at http://www.dekalb.k12.ga.us/druidhills/alumni/history-DHHS.pdf.

103. Chuck Bell, "Briarcliff High to Close, Students Headed for Druid Hills," *Atlanta Journal-Constitution*, August 14, 1986, A/1.

104. Druid Hills High School, "School History," http://www.dekalb.k12.ga.us/druidhills/.

105. Jonathan Harris, "Paideia School Celebrates 25th Anniversary," *Atlanta Journal-Constitution*, June 13, 1996, J/15.

106. The Paideia School, "History," http://www.paideiaschool.org/about_us/history.aspx.

107. Candler, *Asa Griggs Candler*.

108. Dana F. White, "The Hydrangea Effect: Jews Adapt to South," *Atlanta Journal-Constitution*, March 31, 1991, M/4.

109. Alan Patureau, "Putting 'Daisy' on the Map: Druid Hills is Alive with the Sound of Tourists," *Atlanta Journal-Constitution*, March 7, 1990, C/1.

110. Dan Hulbert, "Alfred Uhry's Curtain Call: Writer Reaps Honor at Atlanta Alma Mater," *Atlanta Journal-Constitution*, May 13, 1999, A/1.

Chapter 6: Emory International

111. Bauman, *Warren Akin Candler*.

112. Candler, "An Address Delivered," 10.

113. *Emory Magazine*, Spring 1996.

114. English, *Emory University*.

115. Hauk, *A Legacy*.

116. English, *Emory University*.

117. Hauk, *A Legacy*.

118. Joe Holley, "Ernest Vandiver Jr. Dies; Led GA During Integration," *Washington Post*, February 23, 2005, B0/6.

119. Wagner, "Forging a Unique Partnership."

120. Hauk, *A Legacy*.

121. Ibid.

122. Emory History, "Timeline, 2007," Emory University, http://emoryhistory.emory.edu/timeline/1988.html.

123. Chris Reinolds, "Private Quarters: Owners Restore Builder's Vision," *Atlanta Journal-Constitution*, November 17, 2007, D/3.

124. Alison Young, "Outage Exposes Flaws at CDC Lab," *Atlanta Journal-Constitution*, July 20, 2007, A/1.

125. Craig Schneider, "Crews Blasting 30 Feet From Deadly CDC Germs," *Atlanta Journal-Constitution*, August 16, 2007, A/1.

126. Etheridge, *Sentinel for Health*.

127. Ibid.

128. Ibid.

129. Ibid.

130. Ibid.

131. Mike King, "CDC's eyes on AIDS 25 Years," *Atlanta Journal-Constitution*, June 8, 2006, A/15.

132. Etheridge, *Sentinel for Health*.

133. Jeff Nesmith, "CDC Praised for Anthrax Prevention," *Atlanta Journal-Constitution*, December 7, 2001, A/10.

134. M.A.J. McKenna, "The President in Atlanta: At CDC, Bush Lauds 'New Heroes in America,'" *Atlanta Journal-Constitution*, November 9, 2001, B/1.

135. Jeff Nesmith, "CDC Must Have a Raise, Not Cuts, Chief Tells House," *Atlanta Journal-Constitution*, May 9, 2007, A/3.

136. Urvashk Karkaria, "Atlanta VA Hospital Gets Federal Funding," *Atlanta Business Chronicle*, December 19, 2007.

137. Wheeler, interview.

138. Christy Oglesby, "Office For Veterans Relocates to Decatur," *Atlanta Journal-Constitution*, February 24, 2000, JA/2.

Chapter 7: DHCA

139. Richard Lacayo, "William Levitt," *Time*, December 2, 1998.

140. Smith, "Druid Hills Civic Association," B/1.

141. Ibid.

142. Anne Cowles, "Group Seeks Permit for AIDS Home, Druid Hills Neighbors Say Plan Inappropriate," *Atlanta Journal-Constitution*, March 21, 1989, B/4.

143. Mitchell, *Lewis Edmund Crook, Jr.*

144. Nehl Horton, "Druid Hills Development Planned for Former Paradiso Mansion Site," *Atlanta Journal-Constitution*, February 19, 1987, E/1.

145. Ibid.

146. "Board OK's Zoning Variances for Paradiso Unit," *Atlanta Journal-Constitution*, July 20, 1989, E/13.

147. Mitchell, *J. Neel Reid*.

148. Dr. Marion Kuntz, interview by Robert Hartle, June 28, 2007.

149. Dana F. White, interview by Robert Hartle, June 21, 2007.

150. Bert Roughton Jr., "Presidential Parkway a Giant Step Closer: Appeals Court Upholds Study of Road's Environmental Impact," *Atlanta Journal-Constitution*, December 17, 1987, A/1.

151. Carlson, *At Road's End*.

152. Roughton, "Presidential Parkway," A/1.

153. Bert Roughton Jr., "The Road: 27 Years of Controversy," *Atlanta Journal-Constitution*, September 11, 1988, A/1.

154. Anne Cowles, "Dekalb's Maloof Vetoes Challenge to Parkway," *Atlanta Journal-Constitution*, September 22, 1988, B/1.

155. David Beasley, "Carter Calls Judge Biased About Road, Says Parkway Foes Foiled Bid For Talks," *Atlanta Journal-Constitution*, March 31, 1990, A/1.

156. Lyle V. Harris, "Now, Will Anybody Use the Parkway?" *Atlanta Journal-Constitution*, September 1, 1991, H/1.

157. David Beasley, "Compromise Clears the Way for Parkway, Construction is Likely to Begin by Year's End," *Atlanta Journal-Constitution*, August 29, 1991, A/1.

158. Olmsted, *Civilizing American Cities*.

159. David Pendered, "Parks' Survival Celebrated," *Atlanta Journal-Constitution*, November 1, 2003, G/1.

160. Stacy Shelton, "New Looks for Old Parks: Neighbors Lead Effort to Restore Ponce Green Space," *Atlanta Journal-Constitution*, August 21, 2000, A/2.

161. Olmsted Linear Park Alliance, "OLPA's Past Projects," http://www.atlantaolmstedpark.org/park_past.asp.

162. Mary Macdonald, "Deepdene Work Will Complete Parks Rehab," *Atlanta Journal-Constitution*, February 1, 2007, JB/1.

163. Shelley Emling, "Court-Ordered DeKalb Planning Panel Feels Pressure: Durand Farms Tough Opening Act for Commission," *Atlanta Journal-Constitution*, February 3, 1993, C/4.

164. Shelley Emling, "Durand Farm Developer Countersues Civic Group. Cites Adverse Publicity to Project," *Atlanta Journal-Constitution*, December 2, 1992, C/5.

165. Shelley Emling, "Durand Farm Plan OK'd: Planning Commission Changes Vote After Executive Session," *Atlanta Journal-Constitution*, February 4, 1993, D/2.

166. Shelley Emling, "Court Ordered to OK Developer's Plans," *Atlanta Journal-Constitution*, August 12, 1993, A/1.

167. Katie Baer, "In My Opinion, Development Takes Toll on Trees," *Atlanta Journal-Constitution*, November 3, 1997, A/11.

168. Karen Hill, "In Neighborhood Near Emory, Turkeys Trot at Will," *Atlanta Journal-Constitution*, November 23, 2000, E/1.

169. Mark Davis, "Gobbler Gaggle at Home in Lanes of Druid Hills," *Atlanta Journal-Constitution*, July 17, 2007, E/1.

Bibliography

Bauman, Mark K. *Warren Akin Candler: Conservative as Idealist.* Metuchen, NJ & London: The Scarecrow Press, Inc., 1981.

Boston, Gabriella. "Olmsted Linear Park Set to Turn a New Leaf." *Atlanta Journal Constitution,* August 27, 1998, J0/1.

Bowditch, Eden Unger. *Druid Hill Park: The Heart of Historic Baltimore.* Charleston, SC: The History Press, 2008.

Bryson, Tim. *History of Lullwater.* Lullwater Comprehensive Management Plan. Atlanta: Emory University, 2002.

Candler, Charles Howard. *Asa Griggs Candler.* Atlanta: Foote and Davies, Inc., 1950.

Candler, Warren A. "An Address Delivered by the College of Bishops to the General Conference of the Methodist Episcopal Church, South." *General Conference of the Methodist Episcopal Church, South.* Oklahoma City, OK: Emory University, 1914.

Carlson, Daniel. *At Road's End: Transportation and Land Use Choices for Communities.* Washington, D.C.: Island Press, 1995.

DeKalb County Planning and Developing Department. http://www.co.dekalb.ga.us/planning/mainPage.html.

Dowling, Elizabeth Meredith. *American Classicist: The Architecture of Philip Trammell Shutze.* New York: Rizzoli International Publications, Inc., 1989.

Edge, Sarah Simms. *Joel Hurt and the Development of Atlanta.* Atlanta, GA: Atlanta Historical Society, 1955.

English, Thomas H. *Emory University, 1915–1965: A Semicentennial History.* Atlanta, GA: Emory University, 1966.

Etheridge, Elizabeth W. *Sentinel For Health: A History of the Centers for Disease Control.* Berkeley and Los Angeles: University of California Press, 1992.

Fisher, Irving D. *Frederick Law Olmsted and the City Planning Movement in the United States.* Ann Arbor, MI: UMI Research Press, 1986.

Gournay, Isabelle. *AIA Guide to the Architecture of Atlanta*. Athens: University of Georgia Press, 1992.

Hall, Lee. *Olmsted's America: An "Unpractical" Man and His Vision of Civilization*. New York: Bulfinch Press, 1995.

Hauk, Gary S. *A Legacy of Heart and Mind: Emory Since 1836*. Atlanta: Emory University, 1999.

Jordan, Bruce L. *Murder in the Peach State: Infamous Murders from Georgia's Past*. Atlanta, GA: Midtown Publishing Co., 2000.

Kurtz, Wilbur. "Map of the Battle of Peachtree Creek."

Lyon, Elizabeth A. "Frederick Law Olmsted and Joel Hurt." In *Olmsted South: Old South Critic/ New South Planner*, Dana F. White and Victor A. Kramer. Westport, CT: Greenwood Press, Inc., 1979.

Mitchell, William Robert, Jr. *J. Neel Reid, Architect: Of Hentz, Reid, and Adler and the Georgia School of Classicists*. Atlanta: Georgia Trust for Historic Preservation, 1997.

———. *Lewis Edmund Crook, Jr. Architect 1898–1967: "A Twentieth-Century Traditionalist in the Deep South."* Atlanta, GA: The History Business, 1984.

Olmsted, Frederick Law. *Civilizing American Cities: A Selection of Frederick Law Olmsted's Writings on City Landscapes*. Edited by S.B. Sutton. Cambridge, MA: The Alpine Press, 1971.

———. *Frederick Law Olmsted Papers*. Manuscript Division, Library of Congress, Washington, D.C.

Roth, Darlene R. "Frederick Law Olmsted's First and Last Suburbs: Riverside and Druid Hills." *National Association for Olmsted Parks*. Workbook Series, Vol. 4. 1993.

St. John's Chrysostom Melkite Church. "Candler Mansion." www.stjohnmelkite.org/ candler.html.

Wagner, James W. "Forging A Unique Partnership: CDC, Emory, and Atlanta." *Centers for Disease Control and Prevention*. Atlanta, GA: n.p., 2003.

White, Dana. "Foreword: The Dogwood and the Dollar," In *AIA Guide to the Architecture of Atlanta*, Isabelle Gournay. Athens: University of Georgia Press, 1992.

Zainaldin, Jamil S. "Robert W. Woodruff (1889–1985)." *New Georgia Encyclopedia*. March 23, 2006. http://www.georgiaencyclopedia.org/nge/Article.jsp?id=h-1926 (accessed August 8, 2007).

Visit us at
www.historypress.net